GERMAN PIONEER EQUIPMENT AND VEHICLES

AMPHIBIOUS VEHICLES

Rodolphe ROUSSILLE

Translated from the French by Rodolphe ROUSSILLE

Histoire & Collections

This book was realised under the direction of Raymond Giuliani. Design and lay-out by Antonin Collet.
© Histoire & Collections 2012

A book published by
HISTOIRE & COLLECTIONS
SA au capital de 182 938,82 €
5, avenue de la République F-75541 Paris Cedex 11

Tel : +33-1 40 21 18 20/Fax : +33-1 47 00 51 11
www.histoireetcollections.fr

This book has ben designed typed, laid-out and processed by Histoire & Collections fully on integrated computer equipment.

Photogravure : Studio A & C

Printed in march 2012

by Printworks Int. Ltd (China)

CONTENTS

Special thanks

Special thanks to Stefan De Meyer and the AMC (Archive of Modern Conflict), for their unconditional help
and support with this book, and their wonderful work preserving the photographic heritage
of the Second World War, which they have been doing with passion for years. At (http://ground.warfarethroughthelens.org)
David Fletcher of the Bovington Tank Museum for his invaluable help.
Henry Hoppe, Martin Mace, Karl-Heinz Münch for their help with the illustrations.
Arjan Wiskerke and Danijel Frka for their help identifying the theatres of operations where the L.W.S. saw service.
My publisher Histoire et Collections.
My friend Peter for his help with the English version.
My family, my wife Clotilde, my son Alexandre and my daughter Athénaïs for their support and their patience
during this long project.

I – The beginnings of amphibious vehicles

Autoschiff

Confronted with the development of motorized vehicles after WWI and the emphasis on a war of movement, German engineers had to find new solutions for crossing waterways.

While horses, up until then the principal means of transport for the Cavalry, posed few problems for crossing rivers, the same cannot be said of trucks, tanks and half-tracks.

There were two alternatives available to German engineers: to develop a new system of pontoon bridges and ferries adapted for weight more substantial than horse drawn loads, or to develop amphibious vehicles. Obviously, for technical reasons it was easier to develop a river crossing system based on pontoon bridges and ferries than to make all motor vehicles amphibian.

From the beginning of WWII, certain German tanks were nevertheless equipped with additional systems allowing them to become temporarily amphibious (Panzer II and Panzer 38T) or submersible (The Tauchpanzer : Panzer III, Panzer IV, Panther, Tiger I and Maus). Production of these systems was limited in number and only at certain times: in preparation of Operation Seelöwe (the plan for the invasion of England) or for heavy tanks to cross the river until the development of the J Bridge whose new pontoon system was capable of supporting their increased weight.

With the notable exception of the small car conceived by Ferdinand Porsche and developed by Volkswagen (the Schwimmwagen – 14,000 units), the vast majority of German vehicles during WWII were incapable of crossing waterways.

A variety of crossing systems was developed to equip German engineering troops, the Pioneers. The Pioneers had bridges and pontoon bridges ranging from WWI light type A bridges to type J capable of supporting the weight of Panthers and Tigers.

In parallel to the development of these crossing systems, the design office of the Wehrmacht and certain German companies worked on developing amphibious vehicles for use by the Pioneers. The majority of these vehicles was designed with landings on the English coast in mind. Once this operation was canceled, they were made available to engineering units. They were to serve three main purposes: to transport troops from one bank of a river to the other, to tow landing barges to the beaches during Mediterranean landing operations, and, when they were used by the units of KleinkampfVerbände (German navy commando) at the end of the war, to launch midget submarines to fight off the Allied landings.

A few German manufacturers undertook the elaboration of amphibious vehicles and, thus, had to resolve the problems inherent to this kind of vehicle.

In fact, the body shapes best adapted to navigation are also the least adapted to land travel. In addition, to make them more

mobile on land, it was necessary to make numerous holes in the hull, which inevitably created problems for watertightness and corrosion.

Flotation, stability and maneuverability in water required the development of large, complex structures that were serious handicaps on land. The coexistence of the two systems of propulsion for water and land only increased the technical problems. To be sure, the amphibious vehicle is a technical challenge but inevitably the result of a poor compromise, never totally satisfactory in either element.

Two images of the Autoschiff circulating in the centre of the city, a curious-looking hybrid machine, a cross between a boat and a truck (AMC Collection)

The Germans first creations in this domain were from the end of the 1920s to the beginning of the 1930s. The first known initiative was that of German engineers Hoppe and Krooss, who in 1929 designed for the Reichwehr a four wheel drive vehicle called the "Autoschiff". It looked exactly like a small boat with four wheels added on.

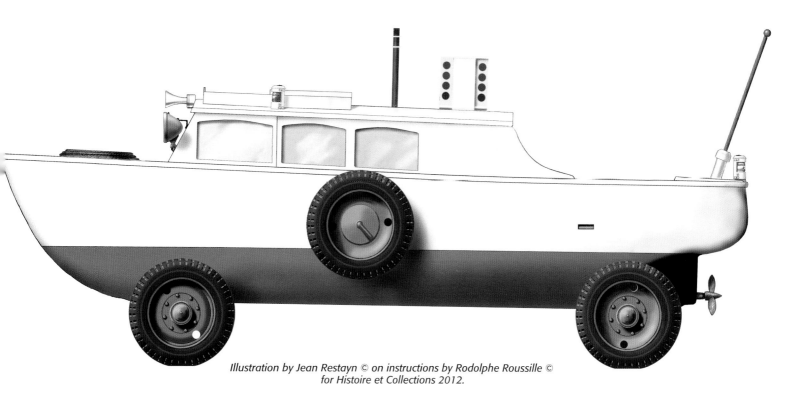

Illustration by Jean Restayn © on instructions by Rodolphe Roussille © for Histoire et Collections 2012.

Two images of the Trippelwagen SK8 during trials. In the first photograph we can see Hans Trippel accompanied by his wife and mother and high ranking Nazi officers. *(AMC Collection)*

II – Trippelwagen
The beginning of the amphibious car

A large part of the history of the German amphibious vehicle was written by the engineer Hans Trippel. Hans Trippel was born on July 19, 1908 in the suburbs of Darmstadt and died on June 30, 2001 in Berlin. He will forever be remembered as one of the pioneers and global experts of amphibious cars of his time.

A professional race car driver at age 26, Hans Trippel quickly became interested in the design of cars. In 1934 he designed his first prototype : an amphibious version of a racing car called the Land Wasser Zeep, based on the chassis of the DKW-F2. The following year, he built another racing car, but this time without amphibious capability.

The same SK8 at the Brandenburg Gate in the centre of Berlin. (AMC Collection)

During the same year, he developed his third vehicle (and second amphibious vehicle), the Land Wasser Zeep Versuchswagen 3. This car was shown to Hitler in December 1935. From this day on, Trippel was officially supported by the German army, with the Heereswaffennamt (Procurement office of the German army), directing him to continue his work to study the development of the concepts for military purposes.

Thanks to the financial support of the Army and a series of constant technical advances by Hans Trippel, the Trippelwagen prototypes improved throughout the years. The Versuchswagen model 4 and 5 with the engine placed in the central position were created in 1936, followed by the Trippel SG6 (Schwimmfähiger

Geländewagen 6), which was the first model in the series. Two years later, Trippel tested his new civilian amphibious car, the SK8. This two wheel drive car was powered by a 2 litre Adler engine and was equipped with a 3 person bench seat. In the following years, two other models of the SG6 were developed: the SG6 Pioneer in 1938 and the SG6/41 in 1941. Two other Trippelwagen prototypes were introduced in 1938: the SG7, fitted with a V8 Tartra engine, and the Kabinenschlitten, a kind of hybrid between a car and a hovercraft powered by airplane propellers.

The first Trippelwagens were produced in Germany at the Homburg/Saar plant. Later, in 1940, production was moved to the Buggati plant in Molsheim in the Bas-Rhin department of France.

The prototype of the hard top SG6, a prototype which never went into production. All later Trippels didn't have roofs either. *(AMC Collection)*

The various versions of the SG6 were the only amphibious cars produced by Trippel for military use during WWII. It was originally designed for use by Pioneers and SS Special Forces. Despite its great reliability and its amphibious and all terrain capabilities, the SG6 was neglected in favor of the Schwimmwagen, which was smaller and less expensive to manufacture.

Official figures show a daily production of six vehicles, equalling a total production of 800-1000 cars by the end of the war undoubtedly a gross exaggeration. The rare photographs that exist tend to prove that the car was used infrequently in the different theaters of operation; most of the photos were taken during test drives.

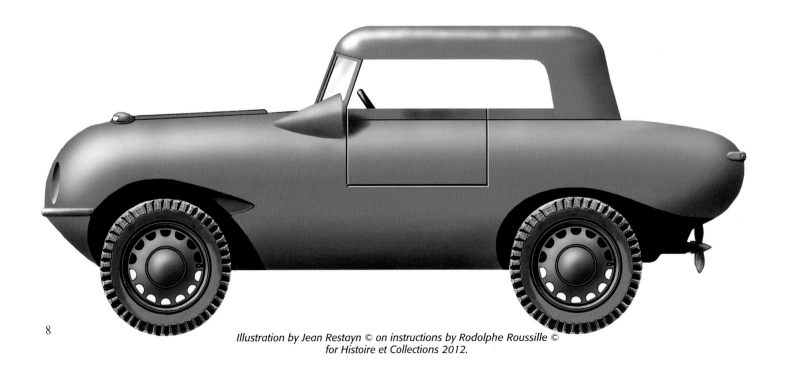

Illustration by Jean Restayn © on instructions by Rodolphe Roussille ©
for Histoire et Collections 2012.

The Trippel SG6

The Trippel SG6 is the first model in the series produced between 1936 and 1937 used by the Wehrmacht. The SG6 was a four wheel drive car powered by an Adler engine and was distinguished by its curved features and complete absence of doors. It had a convertible roof, although a hard-roofed version was tested but not produced in the series.

*Illustration by Jean Restayn © on instructions by Rodolphe Roussille ©
for Histoire et Collections 2012.*

A wrecked Trippel SG6, easily recognizable by its peculiar curved shape. *(AMC Collection)*

WH-695347

The Trippel SG6 Pionier

The Trippel SG6 Pioneer was produced between 1938 and 1943. This wider and elongated version of the SG6 was theoretically able to carry up to sixteen pioneers. It copied the design of the SG6 with the addition of two half-doors, a rear platform and air intakes for the engine. In the Pioneer version, the Adler engine was replaced by an Opel engine and, like the SG6, it was convertible. Today, there are at least two restored models of the SG6 belonging to private collectors.

A rear view of a Trippel SG6 Pioneer entering the water, recognizable by its large rear platform. *(AMC Collection)*

⚡⚡ - 200919

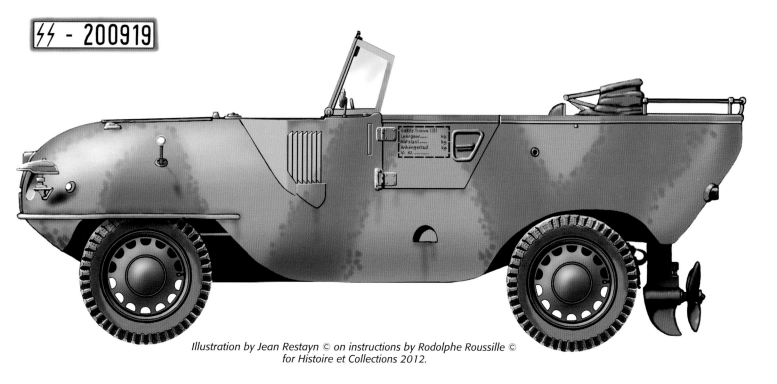

*Illustration by Jean Restayn © on instructions by Rodolphe Roussille ©
for Histoire et Collections 2012.*

Images of the Trippelwagen are rare but a SG6 Pioneer in three-ton camouflage is even rarer.
(AMC Collection)

Another Trippel, a covered SG6 Pioneer on the Russian Front. *(AMC Collection)*

In this picture we can clearly see the relatively high waterline of the Trippel, which really was a good amphibious vehicle. *(AMC Collection)*

A Trippel SG6 Pioneer in the mud being pushed by its crew.
(Collection Karl-Heinz Münch)

Two images of a Trippelwagen SG6 Pioneer belonging to a SS unit. *(AMC Collection)*

The Trippel SG6/41

The SG6/41 was produced between 1941 and 1944 and, like the SG6 Pioneer, was equipped with an Opel engine. With a more streamline shape than her predecessor and the removal of the two half-doors, the SG6/41 represented a return to the original concept. A civilian model, the Kolonialpionier, was developed based on the SG6/41. Today, there remain at least three Trippel SG6/41 : one in France at the Tank Museum in Saumur, and two (including an extremely rare hard-roofed prototype) in the UK at the heart of the famous Wheatcroft Collection.

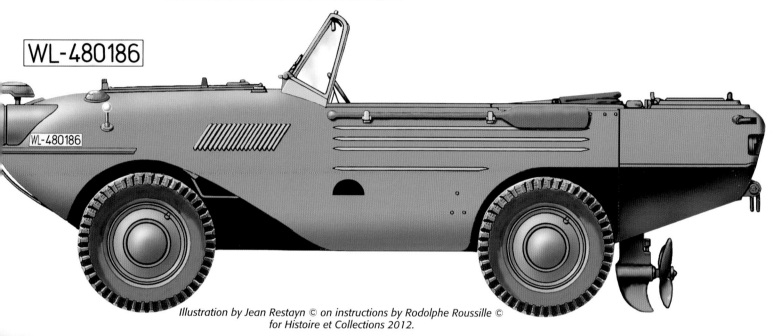

WL-480186

WL-480186

Illustration by Jean Restayn © on instructions by Rodolphe Roussille © for Histoire et Collections 2012.

Photo of a Trippelwagen SG6/41 during trials. (RR)

A Trippel SG/41 leaving the water, with chains on its wheels. This shot was probably taken on the Eastern Front. *(AMC Collection)*

A Trippel SG6/41 being studied by two Russians. *(Collection Karl-Heinz Münch)*

Opposite, below and following page.
Three shots of the same SG /41.
(AMC Collection)

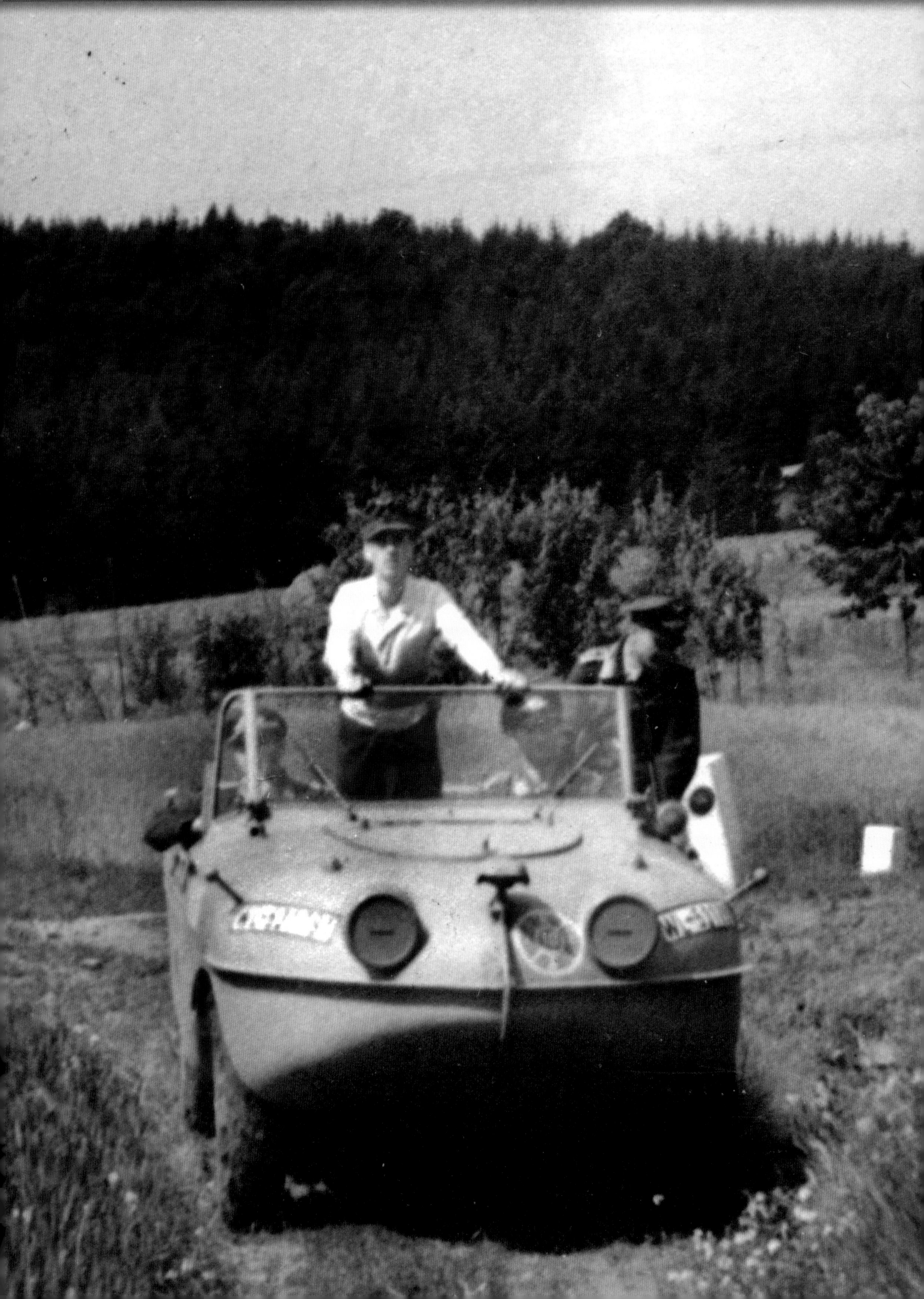

A Trippel SG6/41 driven by an officer during evaluation trials.
(AMC Collection)

WL-531791

WL-531791

Illustration by Jean Restayn © on instructions by Rodolphe Roussille ©
for Histoire et Collections 2012.

Two shots of the Trippel SG6/41 beeig tested by Hans Trippel himself. *(Collection AMC)*

III - Land Wasser Schlepper

Development of the L.W.S.

On January 7, 1941, Major Harvey Smith, military attaché posted to the Embassy in Berlin, wrote a report based on an interview he had had with a former naval officer who had had a strange meeting near Lake Wannsee, on the road from Potsdam to Hamburg.

The officer had come across what he thought to be an amphibious tank doing a 180 degree turn. The description of this perfectly matched that of a similar vehicle seen a few months earlier in Southern Germany. This strange looking vehicle made another appearance almost three months later, on March 31, 1941, parked on a street in the heart of Berlin. It was the subject of a second report. Major Smith reported that no one was allowed to get within 20 meters of the vehicle, the police protecting the security perimeter against any curious on-lookers. Despite the heavy security, a first rough sketch was drawn. In a rather simplistic style, this report described a type of tracked boat with three funnels, large windows at the front for windshields and mentioned a winch and the presence of a rear propeller. This short, but fairly precise description indicates that the officer had come across an early type of Land Wasser Schlepper (L.W.S.), that is to say one of three early versions (L.W.S. 2 99, L.W.S. 3 00, or L.W.S. 4 15). Its dimensions were roughly estimated to be 3.65 meters high and 7 meters long. The report concluded that the vehicle evidently was not an assault tank but was more likely designed to tow pontoon ferries or landing crafts.

The Land Wasser Schlepper or, literally translated, "Land Water Tractor" is one of the most singular vehicles developed by the German army during WWII. This colossus, measuring 8.5m long, 3m wide and 3.15m tall, weighed almost 15 tons. It was equipped with a water-cooled Maybach HL 120 TRM V12 petrol engine with a maximum of 300 horsepower at 3000 rpm, similar to the engine found in the Panzer IV of the time. The engine allowed for a speed of 40 km/h on land and 12.5 km/h in the water, thanks to its two 80 mm diameter propellers.

The origins of the L.W.S. go back to 1935. At this time, the Germany army was starting to seriously think about the possibility of

amphibious vehicles for the purpose of river crossings and beach landings. Section 5 put out an offer to German companies for the development of an amphibious tractor. The vehicle's functional specifications defined its mission as the landing of troops and assistance in aquatic environments. There was to be no offensive or defensive weapon system, but, to fulfill its mission, it was to be equipped with a large cabin and a powerful winch system.

A first prototype was built, and three other LWS followed and were completed during the year 1940. The Land-Wasser-Schlepper was tested repeatedly. A first series of tests took place in August 1940 on the island of Sylt, the northernmost island of the German North Sea. The LWS proved disappointing because of a poor record at sea and because it represented too large of a target in the event of a beach landing. LWS 2 99 and 3 00 were then sent to Oostende, Panzer-Abteilung (Flamm) 100 to be tested again in September 1940, just months after the occupation of Belgium, as part of the training exercises for Operation Seelöwe (Sea Lion, codename for the operation for the invasion of England).

Here, they proved their effectiveness as tug for towing non-motorized barges, freeing vehicles stuck on the beach, and ferrying vehicles and equipment between ships and the shore with their specially designed 10 and 20 ton amphibious trailers. It appears that the LWS had no other practical function and was never used as an offensive element during a beach landing. All of the photos available to date show it completely unarmed in peaceful scenes: on roads and railways, inside landing crafts, towing trailers, barges or launching midget submarines. Subsequent tests were carried out in 1941, particularly with the numbers 4 15 and 5 26 on the island of Wolin the south of the Baltic Sea, off the coast of Pomerania. The construction of almost all of the LWS probably took

> **Photo of the prototype with its large front windows, its small front mudguard and its specific funnel. It has only seven wheels instead of eight for the later versions. It will be transformed later in the war into L.W.S. 1 98.** *(Collection Tank Museum Bovington)*

*Illustration by Jean Restayn © on instructions by Rodolphe Roussille ©
for Histoire et Collections 2012.*

place between 1941 and 1942, but no specific source allows for the dating of the production of each known vehicle.

Construction of LWS involved many German companies. The LWS was developed in 1936 under the direction of the Borsig AG Rheinmetal firm in conjunction with the WaPrüf 5. The company Almärkische Kettenfabrik GmbH supplied the propulsion components and the running gear, and rubber for the wheels and the return rollers were supplied by the tire manufacturer Continental. Gebrüder Sechsenberg AG of Dessau-Rosslau built the superstructure : hull and body. The engine came from the factory of Maybach Motorenbau GmbH of Friedrichshafen and the decoupling system for the transmission and propulsion propellers was supplied by Zahnradfabrik, also based in Friedrichshafen. Various parts were also supplied by the Hüttenwerke firm, located in Sonthofen. The number of LWS constructed and the chronology of their production is difficult to establish given the irregular and often contradictory sources.

Post-war publications state that there were a total of twenty-one vehicles produced : seven pre-production and fourteen production vehicles. In 1941, the official records of the Wehrmacht mention for the first time the existence of three LWS on active duty and another seven newly available as of November. After December 1942, no other LSW was recorded as appearing on active service. Furthermore, the construction of fourteen other nits seems to have been scheduled at this time, but, from that date, all entries for the production of new LWS disappeared from the official records of the Wehrmacht. The exact number of LWS produced is still unknown; however, it is certainly not twenty-one units but more likely between twelve and sixteen.

To this day, the numbering of the different LWS remains a mystery. Some military historians believe that the complex matriculation of LWS was for the sole purpose of concealing from the Allies the true number manufactured. Taking a closer look at the pictorial sources available, we realize that their numbers conceal a subtlety: the first digit is always detached from the other two and is of a larger size. For the LWS 300, for example, we shouldn't read three hundred but three zero zero (LWS 3 00). The first figure is the true number manufactured while the two others seem to have no special significance but to deceive the enemy.

The photographic documentation to which we have access (fifteen foreign language publications, public military archives, and private papers belonging to collectors) includes a total of over three hundred pictures of the LWS, yet shows only a very small number of units produced. The same numbers reappear and we have therefore counted only twelve in total (thirteen if we consider that 2 34 is different number from SER 234). They are: 1 98, 2 99, 3 00, 4 15, 5 26, 6 67, 7 68, 10 71, 11 72 and numbers WM-29 789 (SER 235), WM-29 792 (RES 234) and WM-29 793. Various sources mention the existence of three other LWS: numbers 8 69, 9 70, and 12 21. Unfortunately, our research has not found any photographic evidence confirming the validity of this information. This, of course, does not mean that they do not exist. It is also possible that the numbers WM-29 790 and 791 also existed.

Another possibility is that the later numbers are in fact older, recycled numbers from preproduction models or early series used in later versions. The total production of LWS during the war, therefore, ranges between twelve and sixteen units.

Different Types of LWS

Unlike most of Germany's WWII vehicles, such as half-tracks and tanks that were developed in many versions and listed and inventoried over the years, the LWS has never been the subject of a serious study of its different variants, and understandably so. There are many reasons why it is very difficult to draw up a precise typology of the different models of the LWS.

Documentary sources are almost non-existent, the LWS were produced over a short period of time, and there were many different models (at least six, counting the re-designed prototype, on a photographically proven production of twelve vehicles). Further difficulty arises from the fact that some LWS, like numbers 1 98, 3 00, 4 15, 5 26 and 11 72, underwent many changes during the war. Only careful study of existing iconographic sources enables us to establish a kind of typology; the resulting methodology being to identify a type when more than two similar vehicles were produced. On this basis and by following the numbering of vehicles by way of a chronology of production, we are able to identify three types of LWS : a preproduction or early version, a middle series version, and a late series version. The preproduction version included 2 99, 3 00 and 4 15; the production version included 6 67, 7 68 and 10 71; and the late version included WM-29 789, WM-29 792 and WM-29 793 and the versions of 3 00 and 11 72 modified during the conflict.

Land Wasser Schlepper
Technical description

Most of what we know about the technical characteristics of the LWS comes from an evaluation
performed on LWS 234 by British and American intel-
ligence services after the war. These reports appear
in full below. Only one LWS was photographed during
post-war trials: number 234. Its real plate number
still remains a mystery.

■ General description
The LWS is an amphibious vehicle propelled in the water by
two props combined with twin rudders and driven on land by
caterpillar tracks.
The LWS is of light, riveted construction, generally boat shaped, unarmored and unarmed. It has a deck with a superstruc-

ture, similar to a launch, built up from it, forming the enclosed
crew compartment.
There are hatches in the roof and the rear of the crew compartment; the rearmost hatch in the roof is situated over the engine
and is large enough to access the engine for repairs. All hatches
on the deck or the superstructure are fitted with clamps that en-
sure waterproofness for the rubber joints.
The crew compartment can accommodate twenty men but
with no one standing upright due to the low ceiling. More troops
can be transported outside. The floor of the crew compartment
is very thin and does not allow for transport of cargo. Inside the
cabin is a power-driven bollard winch (plate 5) that receives a 1.5
inch steel cable connected to an exterior, quick-release towing
hook running on a curved track at the rear of the superstructure.

There is also a spring-mounted hook suitable for towing on land.

The engine is mounted aft of centre and drives forward through the radiator, which extends across the hull, to a transfer box, a clutch, and a 5 speed and reverse gearbox similar in externals to that fitted to the Panzerkampfwagen IV. The propeller gear boxes on either side are driven from the transfer box. The vertical spindle fan is also driven from the transfer box, and the power bilge pump is driven from the port shaft to this propeller gearbox.

The drive to the bevel box and final drives is also similar to that on German Panzer IV tanks, but in this case there are no universal joints in the cross shaft. They are placed just aft of the front compartment's bulkhead to the front compartment.

The two sets of brakes are concentric with the cross shaft and placed next to the hull side.

The drive to the winch is from the rear end of the crankshaft to the winch gearbox at the rear of the engine compartment and between the propeller tunnels.

The propeller shafts go through glands accessible from the engine compartment on either side of the engine.

All machinery is placed under the crew compartment floor.

A vertical funnel goes through the forward part of the crew compartment and projects beyond the roof of the superstructure. The forward part of this is a lookout post with no direct access to the interior. The rear part of the funnel forms the cooling air outlet. A cover is provided to fit over the opening.

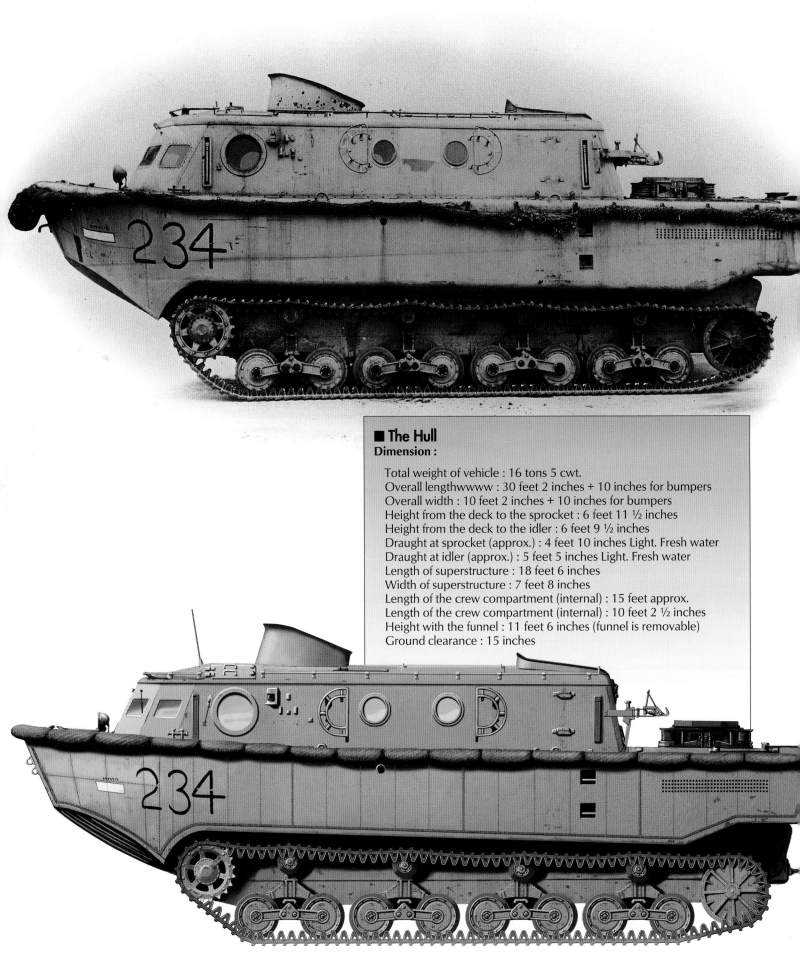

■ The Hull
Dimension :

Total weight of vehicle : 16 tons 5 cwt.
Overall lengthwwww : 30 feet 2 inches + 10 inches for bumpers
Overall width : 10 feet 2 inches + 10 inches for bumpers
Height from the deck to the sprocket : 6 feet 11 ½ inches
Height from the deck to the idler : 6 feet 9 ½ inches
Draught at sprocket (approx.) : 4 feet 10 inches Light. Fresh water
Draught at idler (approx.) : 5 feet 5 inches Light. Fresh water
Length of superstructure : 18 feet 6 inches
Width of superstructure : 7 feet 8 inches
Length of the crew compartment (internal) : 15 feet approx.
Length of the crew compartment (internal) : 10 feet 2 ½ inches
Height with the funnel : 11 feet 6 inches (funnel is removable)
Ground clearance : 15 inches

*Illustration by Jean Restayn © on instructions by Rodolphe Roussille ©
for Histoire et Collections 2012.*

Three views of LWS 234 captured by the British. All its equipment: anchor, buoy and tools have been removed.
(Tank Museum Bovington)

Three views of LWS 234 captured by the British. All its equipment: anchor, buoy and tools have been removed.
(Tank Museum Bovington)

Description :

The hull is made of metal plates, measuring 1/16 to 1/8 inch in thickness, riveted together and reinforced by riveted, steel sections. Each plate is double-riveted.

The hull plating is reinforced by shaped angle pieces with rounded corners. The front and underside of the hull are reinforced by 8 V-shaped tracks distributed the length of the vehicle. Internal stiffeners are placed along the sides, made of straight metal bars and U sections riveted vertically every 12 to 15 inches.

The hull has four principal reinforcement bays, placed lengthways and evenly spaced across the hull's floor. The two outer beams support the suspension brackets and the two center beams support the engine and the gearbox. These beams are supported by lighter metal sections placed longways at regular intervals. The hull is further braced by the crew compartment floor cross beams, and the floor itself is made of light, anti-skid metal plates.

The only bulkheads in the hull are those that shut off the front compartment and the rear compartment, the first containing two connected petrol tanks and the other the winch, rudder gear and two additional petrol tanks.

The hull is provided with two steps on either side, at the rear of the LWS.

The L.W.S
tested by the British

The L.W.S 234 tested at sea by a group of British officers in charge of its technical evaluation. The sea trials were disappointing. *(Tank Museum Bovington)*

Land Wasser Schlepper

The L.W.S 234 is inspected by two British officers. *(RR)*

This profile view of L.W.S 234 with a meter ruler gives a good idea of its impressive dimensions. *(Nara)*

30

The fuel tanks of L.W.S 234 under inspection by a British officer. *(RR)*

■ Control instruments (Photos 1 à 4)

Temperature gauge 30 – 160 ° C	Engine oil
Temperature gauge 25 – 115 ° C	Radiator
Temperature gauge 30 – 160 ° C	Port propeller gearbox
Temperature gauge 25 – 160 ° C	Starboard propeller gearbox
Temperature gauge 30 – 160 ° C	Transfer box
Temperature gauge 30 – 160 ° C	Gear box

Tachometer 1000 – 3200 round per minute, 2600 r.p.m up in red
Speedometer 0 – 60 k.p.h.
Pressure gauge 0 - 0,12 kg/cm². Engine oil
Petrol gauge 0 – 280 litres.
3 position petrol gauge switch, forward tanks, two aft tanks.
The control panel includes the following instruments:

The gear lever is on the right and has five forward speeds and one reverse speed. The clutch pedal is on the left, accelerator on the right and the footbrake, which acts on an independent brake drum on the bevel box, in the centre.

The right and the left hand steering tillers have three positions, forward for normal drive, centre for free turns and rearward for skid turns. They can also be used as parking brakes locked on by a ratchet with a press catch.

The outer set of levers control the screws. In neutral position the levers are vertical. Forward gives forward drive to that screw, rearward gives reverse. Each screw is individually controlled by its own gearbox.

The steering wheel operates the rudders through chains and light steel cables. It may be pulled out or pushed in flush with the panel.

The electric panel is supplied by Bosch, it contains the magneto switch, horn button, starter button with warning light in it, ignition lock, fuse box and various other miner switches for lamps at many points.

■ Engine (Photo 5)

The engine is a 300 h.p. Maybach HL 120, as used in the Panzer IV.

It is fitted with an inertia starter driven by handle from the rear of the superstructure on the port side and clutched in by the driver through a control on his left. It has also an electric starter.

Two exhaust pipes extend to the rear of the vehicle with large silencers fitted on either side and expansion pieces fitted at the manifold. The exhaust silencers are effective.

■ Speed in gears (Rear from Rev. Counter and speed)

Gear	R.P.E.	Speed
1	-	-
2	2600	3.0
3	2600	6.0
4	2600	8.7
5	2600	12. nt0

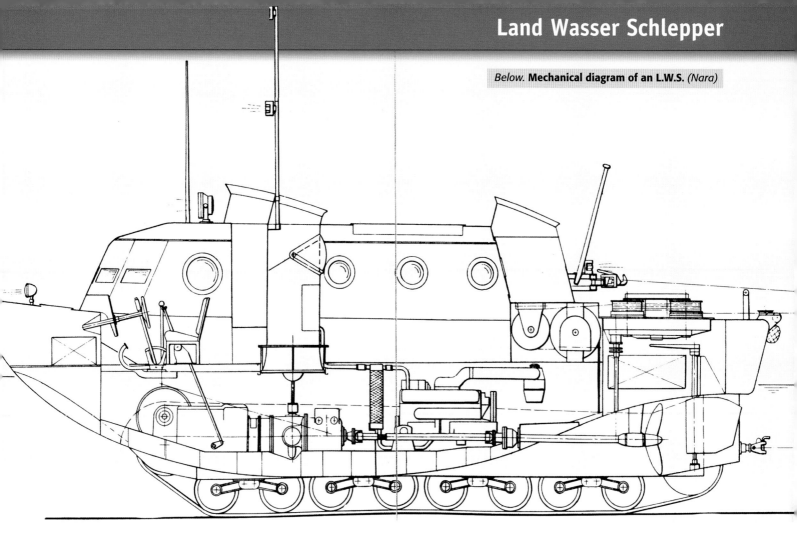

Below. **Mechanical diagram of an L.W.S.** (*Nara*)

■ Steering brakes and final drives (Photo 6)

The method of steering is cultch brake with a sun and planet type of gear similar to the Panzer IV. They are air cooled by 3 inches pipe leading to the forward compartment. The brake housings are different from the MK.IV.

The final drive is bolted up from the outside of the vehicle through the hull to the brake assembly.

■ Cooling fan

The cooling fan is driven by a vertical shaft from the transfer box. It extracts air from the engine compartment through the radiator and send it out through the 24 inch diameter funnel.

Fan dimensions :

Outside diameter	24 inches
Hub diameter	14 ½ inches
No. Of blades	4
Pitch of blades	30 inches
Axial dimension	7 ½ inches
Inlet	Bell mouth with vanes
Material	Steel

Photo 5. **In this picture we can see the L.W.S. engine a Maybach 120 TRM V12 the same used on the Panzer IV. The engine was located inside the crew compartment under the floor just before the Funnel. The crew could access the motor by removing two panels on the floor. Two hatches were located on the roof just under the engine, in case of a removal or repairs.**
(*Tank Museum Bovington*)

Photo 6. **An interesting shot of the steering gear and side brakes; it is similar to those fitted on the Panzer IV. In this shot we can see that this equipment was located just between the driver's seat, radio operator's seat and the funnel.**
(*Tank Museum Bovington*)

Photo 7. **This lookout post located in the funnel was only fitted on the middle and late models of the LWS. At the rear of the funnel you can see the tube for the air outlet coming from the radiators.** *(Tank Museum Bovington)*

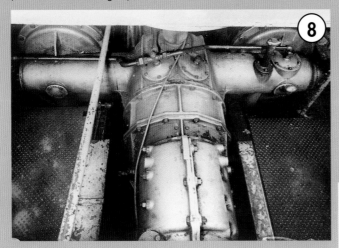

Photo 8. **Details of the separate transfer box and propeller gear boxes.** *(Tank Museum Bovington)*

Photos 9 et 10. **Rear pictures showing the two huge L.W.S. 800 mm diameter propellers, and their twin rudders.** *(Tank Museum Bovington)*

Photo 11. **Detail of the hook and of the winch system located on the rear deck.** *(Tank Museum Bovington)*

■ Radiators ((Photo 7)

The cooling air circuit is from openings on either side of the winch control platform to the aft end of the engine compartment, through this to the radiators and out through the fan funnel. The cooling would be completely upset if any of the trap doors forward of the radiator was opened.

The radiator filler is in the funnel.

Dimensions	
Width	6 feet 4 inches
Depth	2 feet 3 ¾ inches
Matrix thicknes	5 ¾ inches

■ Propellers and drives (Photos 8, 9 & 10)

The drive to each propeller gearbox is from either side of the transfer box through bevel gears and cross shafts. The gearboxes are axially disposed and drive the shafts which pass aft on either side of the engine to glands through the hull to the propellers. The gearboxes have forward and reverse speeds and neutral.

Dimensions	
Number of propellers	3
Rotation	in opposite directions
Propeller diameter	2 feet 7 inches
Tunnel diameter	2 feet 7 inches
Number of blades per propeller	4
Pitch of blades	26 inches
Shaft diameter	2 ¾ inches
Speed forward and reverse	approx 1/5 engine speed

■ Rudders (Photos 9 et 10)

Number of rudders : 2
Position : Behind each screw
Height of rudders : 2 feet 3 ½ inches
Width of rudders : 2 feet 2 inches to 1 foot 9 inches wide

Photo 12. **First type drive sprockets with one row of teeth, fitting early and middle production L.W.S.** *(AMC)*

Photo 13. **Late type drive sprockets, star shaped, with two rows of teeth, which fitted late type and some upgraded early and middle production ones like the L.W.S 300, 4 15 and 1 98.** *(AMC)*

Photo 14. **The idler of the L.W.S was the same as on a version of the Panzer II. This idler was identical to all L.W.S types.** *(Tank Museum Bovington)*

Photo 15. **Bogies with an early type of semi-elliptic springs. This shot was taken on LWS 2 34. Note that this is an exception: On the early models equipped with the same springs, the return rollers are not located just under the bogies because the 2 34 was fitted with 4 return rollers instead of 3 top rollers for the early running gear.**

Photos 16 et 17 **Two shots of a late bogie with single quarter elliptic spring per bogie of two wheels. Two rebound rubber snubbers are fitted.** *(AMC)*

Photo 18. **A wheel and late track link especially designed for the late type L.W.S. We can see the arrow on the wheel indicating the direction of movement.** *(RR)*

Control : Rudders are coupled and controlled from driver's seat or by emergency tiller on deck aft.

■ Suspension, Bogies, Sprockets and Idlers

(Photos 12 à 17)

The Different versions of the Land-Wasser-Schlepper were equipped with several types of running gear, except the L.W.S. 1 98, which was specific as a prototype. For all the other L.W.S. there were four two-wheeled suspension units on either side.

a – The two types of drive sprockets:

The early type had no holes, with only one row of teeth. The shape is similar to some Panzer II drive sprockets.

The late type was star-shaped with holes and a double row of teeth much closer to the shape of some Panzer IV.

b – Idlers

This is the only part which remains unchanged from one version to another. This is also a standardized part coming from the running gear of the Panzer II auf C.

Diameter : 2 feet 4 ½ inches

c- Bogies and suspension units

The bogies:

The bogies with a diameter of 19 ½ inches were riveted on to the side and bottom of the hull with a reinforced hull plate between. The bogie wheels are mounted on separate axle arms facing opposite ways and suspension is by two different types of springs.

The suspension springs:

Contrary to what has been written in the past, military historians have certainly been misled by their observations on the Photographs of L.W.S. 234.The first version of the springs of the L.W.S was a single semi-elliptic spring spanning the bogies. The L.W.S. 2 99, 3 00 and 4 15 were fitted with this type of spring. This type of suspension unit was made of 24 leaves, with a width of leaves of 3 1/16 inches.

The late version was an improved version of these springs. This type of bogie had a single quarter elliptic spring per bogie of two wheels. The wheels were mounted on forked fore and aft radius arms, rebound rubber snubbers were fitted. This suspension appears markedly superior to that fitted on the original vehicle and should have given the vehicle a reasonable cross country performance.

d. Top rollers/ return rollers

There was only one type of top roller; these were also fitted with the rubber made by Continental. On the early and middle production L.W.S there are only 3 return rollers per side, and on the late type there were 4.

It is notable that the running gear of the L.W.S. was subject to constant upgrades. Thus, for example, the rolling gear of L.W.S 3 00 which was at the beginning an early type of running gear (Early type drive sprocket, 3 return rollers, bogies of the first type fitted with the single semi-elliptic springs) received the new type of drive sprocket and late type of tracks between 1942 and 1943.

■ Tracks (Photo 18)

There were two types of tracks; one for each type of Drive Sprocket.

The first type of tracks, which went with the early type of drive sprockets, was in fact the same as that used for the Panzer II. The second version, which went with the late type of drive sprockets, was specifically developed for the late series of LWS.

These track links are cast manganese steel with headed pins, held in place by soft iron wire threaded through the pin and bent over. Pin heads on the inside of the tracks serve as an additional safeguard, and short ramps at the rear and the final drive casing at the front push in any that come loose. The links do not closely resemble closely any other German track but may be of Czech design. The bogies run between the two guide horns.Dimensions

Track centres :	8 feet 5 ½ inches
Length of track on ground	15 feet 3 ½ inches
Ground clearance	15 inches

Rare shot of the inside of the crew compartment of the late type of L.W.S. No other shot of the inside is known. We can see the winch. The tubes attached on the starboard side are used to put the light on the roof in sea configuration
(Tank Museum Bovington)

Track width over pins	13 inches
Number of links per side	143
Track pressure	8.1 lbs. ”in²

■ Winch (Photos 19 et 20)

The winch gearbox incorporates a clutch, high and low speed gear in forward and reverse directions, a neutral position and a brake. ... The drive goes through the bulkhead, to a vertical shaft, and then to the winch.

The winch is of unit construction is completely enclosed.

The rear bollard has 7 grooves with the lowest one being deep; the forward bollard has only 6. Rope clamping brackets and rollers are fitted on both sides. The spare rope goes through a fair-

lead into the crew compartment where it is wound up by hand onto a drum with a ratchet.

Clutch : foot operated
Gearbox : Hand operated. Three positions – IN . Neutral Out
Brake : hand operated
Bollards : forward : one, 6 grooves
Aft : one, 7 grooves
Diameter to root of grooves 14 inches : Pitch of groove : 5/8 inches
Speed of winching AT 1000 r.p.m of engine maximum 26000 safe r.p.m
In or anticlockwise : 8 r.p.m or 31 feet/minute
Out or clockwise : 11 r.p.m or 43 feet / minute

(Tank Museum Bovington)

(DR)

Photos 20 et 21. **Two shots of the opened cabin's rear part of the standard and late type L.W.S.**

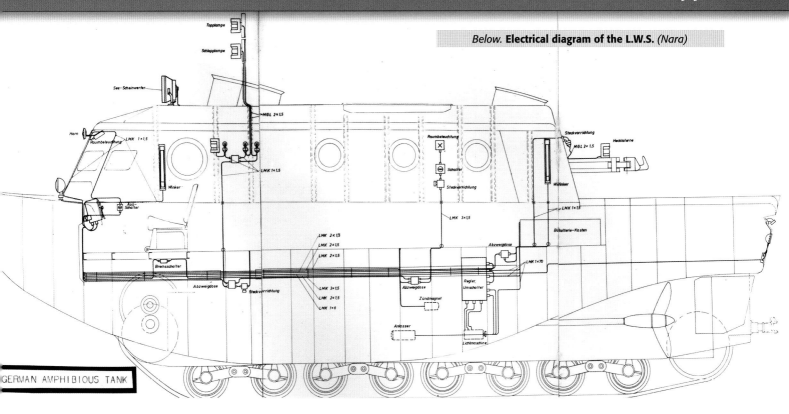

Below. **Electrical diagram of the L.W.S.** *(Nara)*

GERMAN AMPHIBIOUS TANK

Winching in is possible at both speeds but the fairlead to the drum suits the In or Anti-clockwise direction only, giving the slower speed.

■ Bilge pumps

A 2 1/4 inches centrifugal bilge pump driven off the port propeller cross drive shaft discharges through the hull sides.

The pump has 10 suction points with valves that are remote-controlled from a bank of selector levers located in the crew compartment beneath the rope drum.

The 10 suction points are:
- Front compartment : Port front
- Motor compartment : Port rear
- Motor compartment : Starboard front
- Tank compartment : Starboard rear
- Rear compartment : Outer ausch

A dump valve remotely operated by a removable hand wheel in the floor is also fitted.

An emergency semi-rotary hand pump n° 3 size is fitted to the port wall of the crew compartment and is cross connected to the power bilge lines.

■ Electrical fittings.

Four 12-volt batteries are installed below the winch control platform and over the rear end of the engine compartment.

A box is mounted on the starboard side of the engine compartment containing a changeover switch for starting, voltage controller etc. The master switch is fitted above.

There is a box for a wireless set (not fitted) in front of the wireless operator opposite the driver. A complete system of intercommunication to the various stations, such as the winch control platform, and the lookout in the funnel, is fitted.

All the light connections and switches are substantial marine type fittings with blanking caps for all plug points.

■ L.W.S external fittings.

The late types of L.W.S were equipped with radios. Each LWS had its own life-buoy on the starboard side and an anchor with a rope on the port side. The tools were clamped onto the roof of the L.W.S. Several LWS had additional equipment such as small or large boxes for extra life-buoys, rope, crew life-jackets, tools, etc... Sometimes they had extra fuel drums on their external rear platform. Some L.W.S. also had ladders to help crewmembers climb aboard this behemoth.

Photo 22. **Detail of the hook and winch system located on the rear deck.** *(Tank Museum Bovington)*

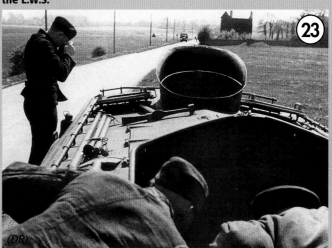

Photo 23. **In this picture we can see the tools clamped to the roof of the L.W.S.**

(DR)

The different LWS identified and their development
The prototype transformed into L.W.S. 1 98

Here under and pages 42, 43.
**Four shots of the crew of the LWS 1 98
taken in front of a Shell gas station.**
(Collection AMC)

The first prototype to emerge was characterized both by a variety of elements later to be found on the three types identified and by elements unique to prototype.

First of all, its hull had a slightly different shape than that of later types. The bow was slightly higher and the size and shape of the iron plates that made up the hull were different. There were no foot holes on the port side, unlike later LWS, and it had foot holes at the front starboard side that were not found on previous LWS. The presence of small mudguards at the front was the final detail differentiating the first hull from the following versions.

The cabin also had its share of peculiarities; the funnel had a specific form reminiscent of those of the ocean liners of the era. The large lateral windows of the windscreen were square shaped whereas on later models there were replaced by large round portholes. Another element unique to the prototype was the absence of the rear winch. Its running gear had its own oddity; the last bogie only had one wheel instead of two, a total of seven wheels for the running gear compare to eight for the LWS series.

After having been tested the prototype underwent conversion and officially became the LWS 1 98. It underwent fresh trials along with three other LWS on a special beach landing training ground in the Baltic coast.

From its conversion the LWs 1 98 only kept a few distinctive element allowing it to be identifiable from the others, the hull with its particular shape and its front mudguards and its unique seven wheels running gear. Its cabin was also modified; the large front windows and the funnel were replaced by standardized parts. The new cabin in fact was practically identical to the two final types down to the last detail except for the three lateral portholes instead of two on the final models. The running gear was upgraded probably between 1940 and 1941 and was equipped with star shaped drive sprocket, as well as the tracks created specifically for the late type LWS. It only had three return rollers instead of the later running gear which had four.

Picture of the L.W.S 1 98, on its left the L.W.S. 4 15. They are both in maintenance after trials.
(Collection AMC)

The L.W.S. 2 99, 3 00 & 4 15 : three early series vehicules

The early series, or Pre-production LWS was characterized by a typical one room cabin. It was equipped with three ventilation funnels, large front windows to which could be affixed detachable steel pierced armour with small portholes, and side faces with a large window at the front followed by three smaller ones. Access to the interior could be gained through the roof (same as on the other versions), or by two small doors also with small windows located at the rear of the cabin. The running gear was of the first type and consisted of a full drive sprocket with a single row of teeth, three return rollers and first type bogies with a single semi-elliptical spring. The tracks used on the undercarriage of the first type were those of PzKpfw II.

Above and next page.
Though taken at various angles, these five pictures of the preproduction L.W.S. are not sharp enough to allow indentifying its serial number. *(Collection AMC)*

L.W.S. 2 99

The L.W.S. 2 99 was delivered to Panzer-Abteilung (Flamm) 100 in August 1940. From here on we lose all trace of it, no contemporary photograph attests to its use after the trials at Oostende. Photographs of the day show it with two-tone camouflage patches, most likely two shades of grey, a dark grey and a light grey as found on the ships of the Kriegsmarine. It is also possible that the camouflage was grey-green in colour.

Wa.Prüf5 IVb
LWS2 99

Wa.Prüf5 IVb
LWS2 99

48

Illustration by Jean Restayn © on instructions by Rodolphe Roussille ©
for Histoire et Collections 2012.

Picture of L.W.S. 2 99 taken in Oostende during trials prior to Operation Seelöwe (operation planned to invade England). *(E.C.P.A.D.)*

Five other crisps photos of L.W.S. 2 99 training for Seelöwe in Ostende. One can cleraly see the curious white insigna painte the right hand side which looks like a mouse towing a box, p● symbolising the main function of the LWS: towing land barges (E.C.P.A.D.)

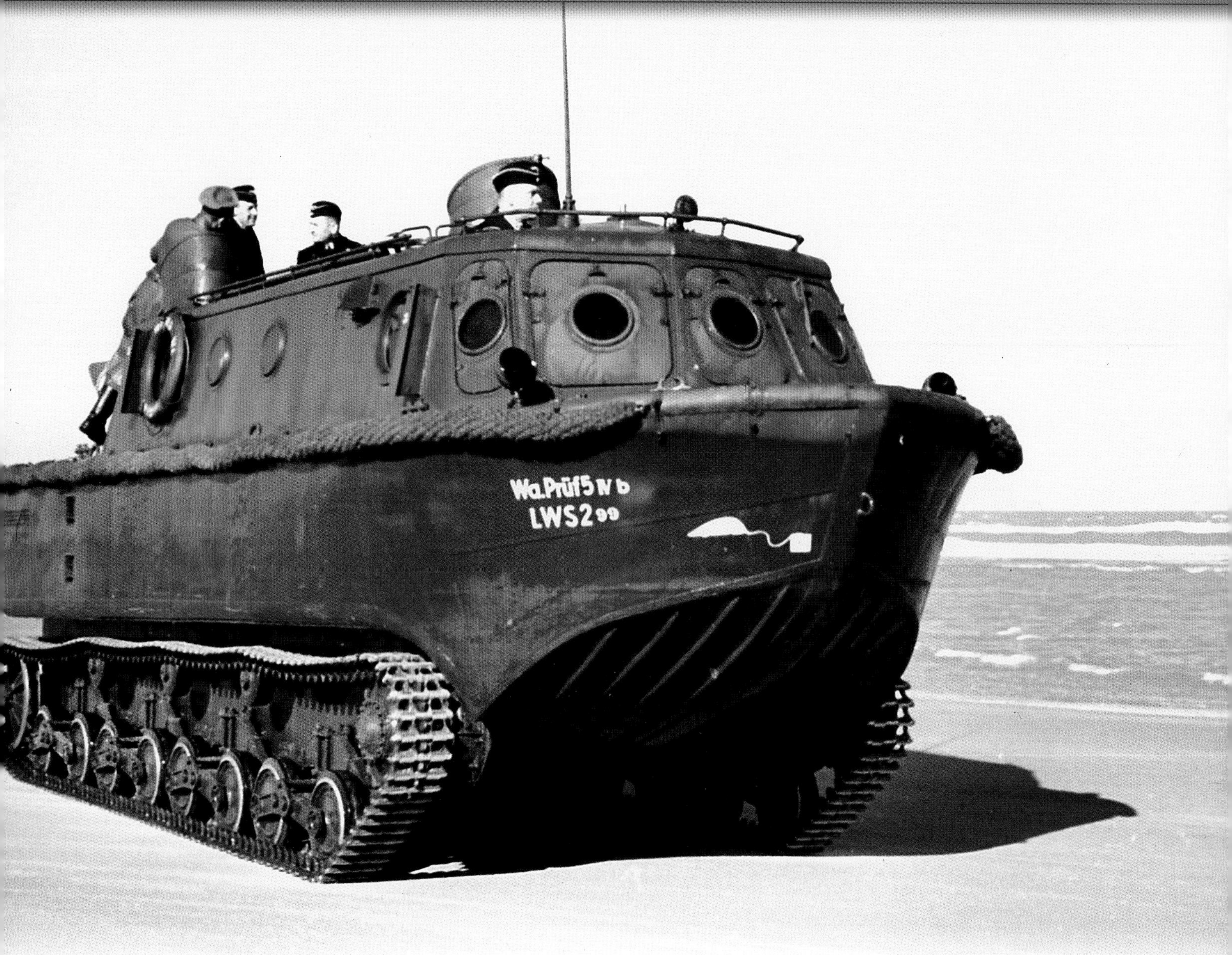
Wa.Prüf5 IV b
LWS2 99

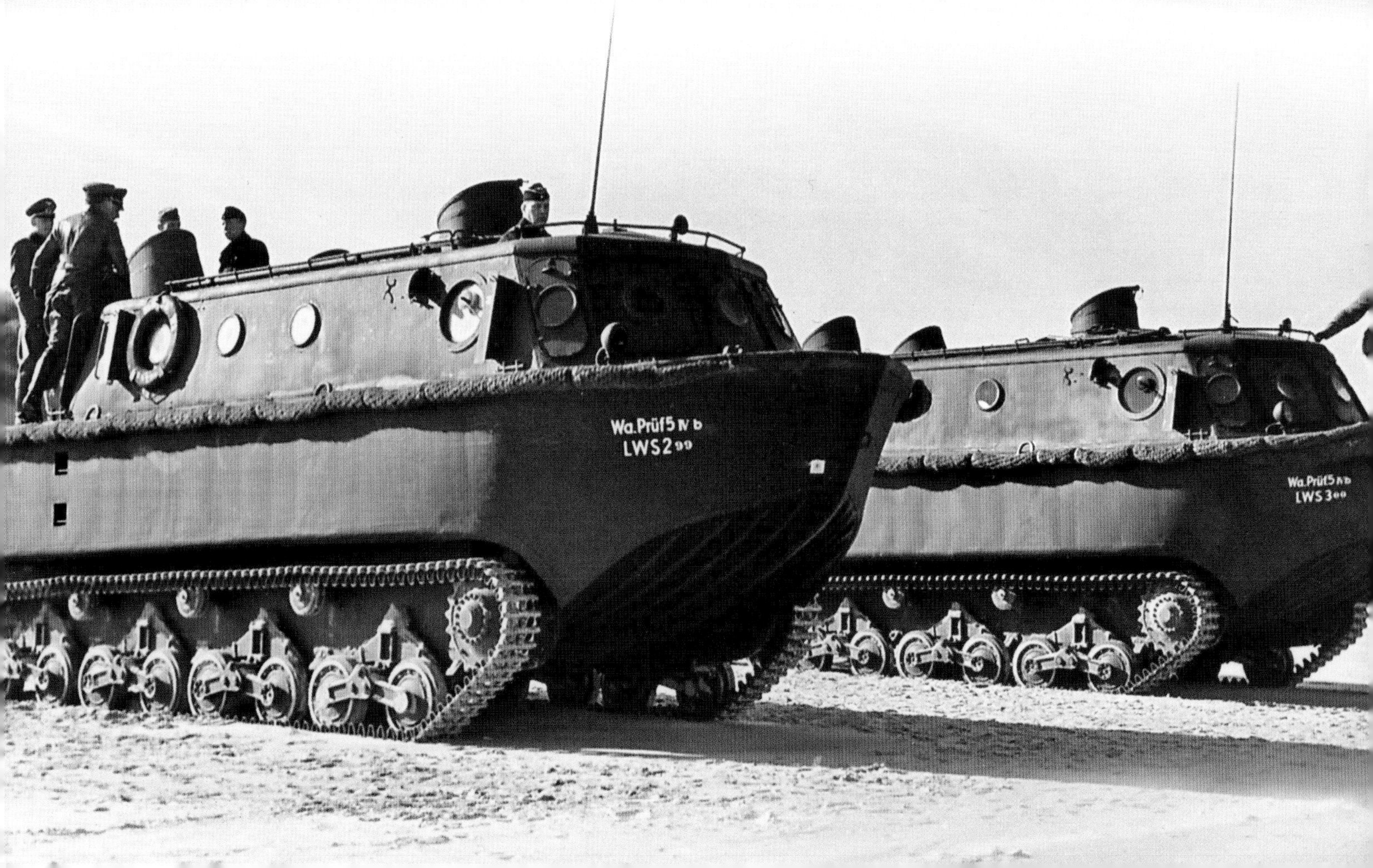
Wa.Prüf5 IV b
LWS2 99
Wa.Prüf5 IV b
LWS3 00

Below and following page above
Three other photos of the LWS 2 99 in Ostende.   The flag was only present for these evaluations, never during an operation(*E.C.P.A.D.*)

The only known photo of the LWS 2 99 not taken in Ostende. We were unable to determine its exact location.
(Collection AMC)

L.W.S. 3 00

Wa.Prüt5 Nb
LWS 3 00

The LWS 3 00 had a longer service history, if not a happier one. Like its twin, it was tested at Panzer-Abteilung (Flamm) 100 and then was sent to Pionier-Landungs-Kompanie 777 in July 1941 where it took part in exercises in the Baltic. Certain post-war publications indicate that it finished its service as part of Pionier-Landungs-Bataillon 86 in May 1943.

At the beginning it was equipped exactly like the L.W.S. 2 99 but it was to be modified several times. A series of photographs, most likely taken in Croatia in 1942-43, show a late version pulling a PionierLandungsBoot Boot type 40 on a beach

These photographs show how heavily modified it was:
A second type star-shaped front sprocket
Late type tracks
A second type cabin with small forward windows

Wa.Prüt5 Nb
LWS 3 00

*Illustration by Jean Restayn © on instructions by Rodolphe Roussille ©
for Histoire et Collections 2012..*

(E.C.P.A.D.)

(E.C.P.A.D.)

However, it retained the three return rollers, the original bogies, and the single blade semi-elliptical suspension.

Camouflage

After the Oostende trials where it was seen with the same two-tone camouflage schema as the 2 99, it seems to have been repainted, most likely a monotone clear grey and possibly a sand colour for Croatia.

It is possible that the L.W.S. didn't finish its career in 1943, but continued on while simply changing its number. The post war evaluation report tells us that construction information on the funnel of the L.W.S. 234 indicated:

Year of Construction: 1940
Model Number: 09/214 / 300

Elsewhere on an electrical panel was the following information:

Enststört nach Gruppe MI / L.W.S. 3 00 / Bosch

55

Same training, this time with L.W.S. 3 00, the camouflage on the L.W.S with big patches made of two colours of grey. *(E.C.P.A.D.)*

Wa.Prüf5 Nb
LWS 3 00

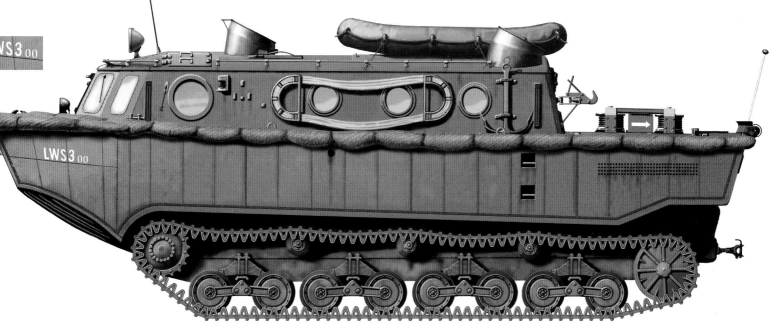

The L.W.S. 3 00 on manoeuvres in the Baltic.

The L.W.S. 3 00 in the Baltic trials towing a German Landing craft N°3 type 39. Towing barges was one of the main tasks of the L.W.S. *(Collection AMC)*

Three more photos of the 3 00 maneuvering in the Baltic. We can see a rubber lifeboat on the roof as on the boats of the Kreigsmarine.
(Collection AMC)

The L.W.S. 3 00 in Croatia.

LWS 3 00

for Histoire et Collections 2012.

**Two Photos of L.W.S. 3 00 in Yugoslavia, probably taken
in Kraljevica. It was completely upgraded, with a new cabin of the
late type, new late drive sprockets and track links.
The camouflage net is impressive.**
(Collection AMC)

Three more photos of the LWS 3 00 towing on the bank a landing barge of type 40 with the number 212. The camouflage net is impressive.*(Collection AMC)*

Another photo taken in Yugoslavia, probably in Kraljevica. The vehicle is completely changed with a series cabin and sprockets and tracks of the second type. *(Collection AMC)*

P

LWS 3 00

LWS 3 00

Illustration by Jean Restayn © on instructions by Rodolphe Roussille © for Histoire et Collections 2012.

L.W.S. 4 15

The L.W.S. 4 15 was assigned to the Pionier-Landungs-Kompanie 540 in April 1942. It, too, was tested in the Baltic. All of the photographs taken of the machine show it as a single colour, probably a medium grey. The fact that there are very few images of LWS leads us to believe that it didn't have a long operational life. .

Four rare pictures of the L.W.S. 4 15 during trials with the Wä.Pruf 5 IVB markings.
(Collection AMC)

L.W.S. 500 26 et 5 26

The L.W.S. 500 26

Above, below and next pages.
Several shots of the L.W.S 5 00 26 on the Eastern Front before it was upgraded. It is a hybrid between the early and middle production types of L.W.S.
(Collection AMC)

This vehicle at first received the matriculation 500 26, then it became the 5 26. The first version of the 500 26 was almost identical to the early series models like the L.W.S. 2 99, 3 00 and 4 15, the exception being the bogies, which were of the second type. Numerous photographs were taken of the L.W.S. 500 26 on the Eastern Front along with two others, L.W.S 6 67 and 7 68 as part of Pioneer battalion 627. It appears that on the Russian Front it was painted a uniform grey.

Above, below and preceeding pages.
Five other photos of L.W.S. 5 00 26 belonging to Pionier Bataillon 627, taken on the Eastern Front before its upgrade to 5 26 versions. This first version is identical to the early version except for its late type suspension.
(Collection AMC)

This first version of the
L.W.S. 500 26 is quite
similar to the early
type but it has the late
type of bogies with the
quarter elliptic springs.
We can see a ladder on
the starboard side to
help crew members to
board this big monster.
(Collection AMC)

Several photos taken during the eastern campaign with the three L.W.S. The L.W.S. 500 26 had engine problems that had obviously required time to be repaired, considering the numerous shots of it being towed by the LWS 6 67.
(Collection AMC)

The 5 26, a hybrid model.

Illustration by Jean Restayn © on instructions by Rodolphe Roussille
© for Histoire et Collections 2012.

The LWS was upgraded before its departure for Cyrenaica. It received a new front windshield with small rectangular windows but retained the characteristics of the early cabin with the three small funnels and three small port holes.
(Collection AMC)

Back from the Russian Front, this vehicle was then sent to Africa. Prior to this, it had already been transformed, as evidenced by photographs taken of it in the winter snow. This vehicle was a mix of the two previous types. The L.W.S. 5 26 was generally inspired by the early models, the only difference being that it was equipped with forward windows (small and rectangular) of the later types and also bogies of the second type. Assigned to the Pionier-Landungs-Kompanie 778 in April 1942, it was one of two LWS, along with LWS 6 67, to be sent to Libya as part of the Afrika Korps and was painted a sand colour, leaving its original grey paint showing in many places.

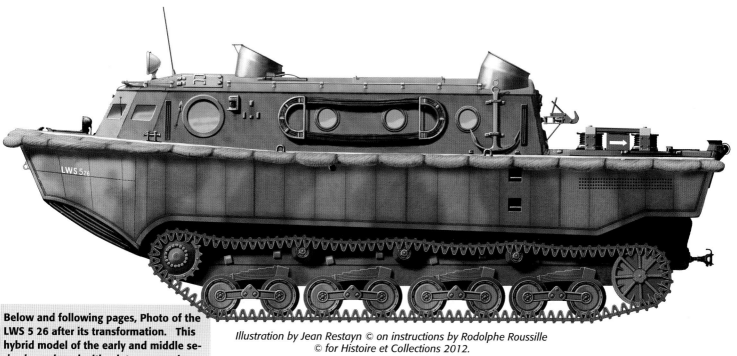

Illustration by Jean Restayn © on instructions by Rodolphe Roussille
© for Histoire et Collections 2012.

Below and following pages, Photo of the LWS 5 26 after its transformation. This hybrid model of the early and middle series is equipped with a late suspension, and an early type cabin with the middle type front windows (small rectangular windows without detachable protection masks). (Collection AMC)

LWS 5 26

Equipping the Pionier-Landungs-Kompanie 778 in April 1942, it was one of the two L.W.S. (with the 6 67) to be sent to Libya with the Afrika Korps. On this occasion it was swabbed roughly with beige paint which allowed the original grey paint to show through it.

Profile illustrating the camouflage pattern of the LWS 5 26 having received a crude distemper of beige with its original grey paint showing through in many places. When the LWS 5 26 was seen with this camouflage in May 1942, it was operating in the Pionier Landungs Batallion 777 in the Azov Sea.

LWS 526

Illustration by Jean Restayn © on instructions by Rodolphe Roussille © for Histoire et Collections 2012.

The Production Version :
The L.W.S 6 67, 7 68 et 10 71

The production version differs in the development of the cabin. The running gear is practically identical, except that new bogies with quarter ellipse suspension blades equipped with small stoppers replace the previous bogies.

The cabin underwent many noticeable changes. Firstly, the three funnels were replaced by a single funnel placed in the front. An observation post, which had no access to the cabin, was attached to part of the funnel. The watchman was obliged to pass by the roof of the cabin to get to the observation post. Next, of the three port holes on the earlier models only two remained on this version. At the rear of the cabin was a hatch (as on the previous model, and which was a double hatch on the first model) that allowed direct access to the main compartment. Finally, the large windshields were replaced by smaller rectangular windows.

The L.W.S. 6 67 on the eastern front

Illustration by Jean Restayn © on instructions by Rodolphe Roussille © for Histoire et Collections 2012.

(Collection AMC)

(Collection AMC)

The L.W.S. 6 67

Just like the LWS 5 26, the LWS 6 67 was originally part of the Pionier Batallion 627 and was then assigned to the Pionier-Landungs-Kompanie 778 in April 1942. It was the most photographed LWS of all of WWII with at least 30-40 photographs depicting it on all of the fronts. One photograph shows it on the Eastern front with its 10 tonne amphibious trailer painted in three-tone camouflage, brown, sand and green. Before leaving for Africa the L.W.S. 6 67 was stationed in Sicily where it received its new insignia of the Pionier-Landungs-Kompanie778, an anchor with two crossed flags and a boat steering wheel. After its arrival in Cyrenaica, it was repainted a sand colour with a wide white stripe on the cabin.

Twenty photos of the L.W.S. 6 67 on the Eastern Front.
It has two additional metal boxes on the rear deck;
it is a good, quick way to identify it. *(Collection AMC)*

Above, below and following pages.
Five shots of L.W.S. 6 67 in the Pionier Bataillon 627. This is a production series machine with the new type of cabin fitted with only two side windows and smaller rectangular front windows.
(Collection AMC)

LWS 667

Above, below and following pages.
Six further shots of the L.W.S. 6 67 on the Eastern Front. The markings – a big white K and the Pionier Bataillon 627's insignia – were painted on the hull, left-hand side at the front and right at the rear. *(Collection AMC)*

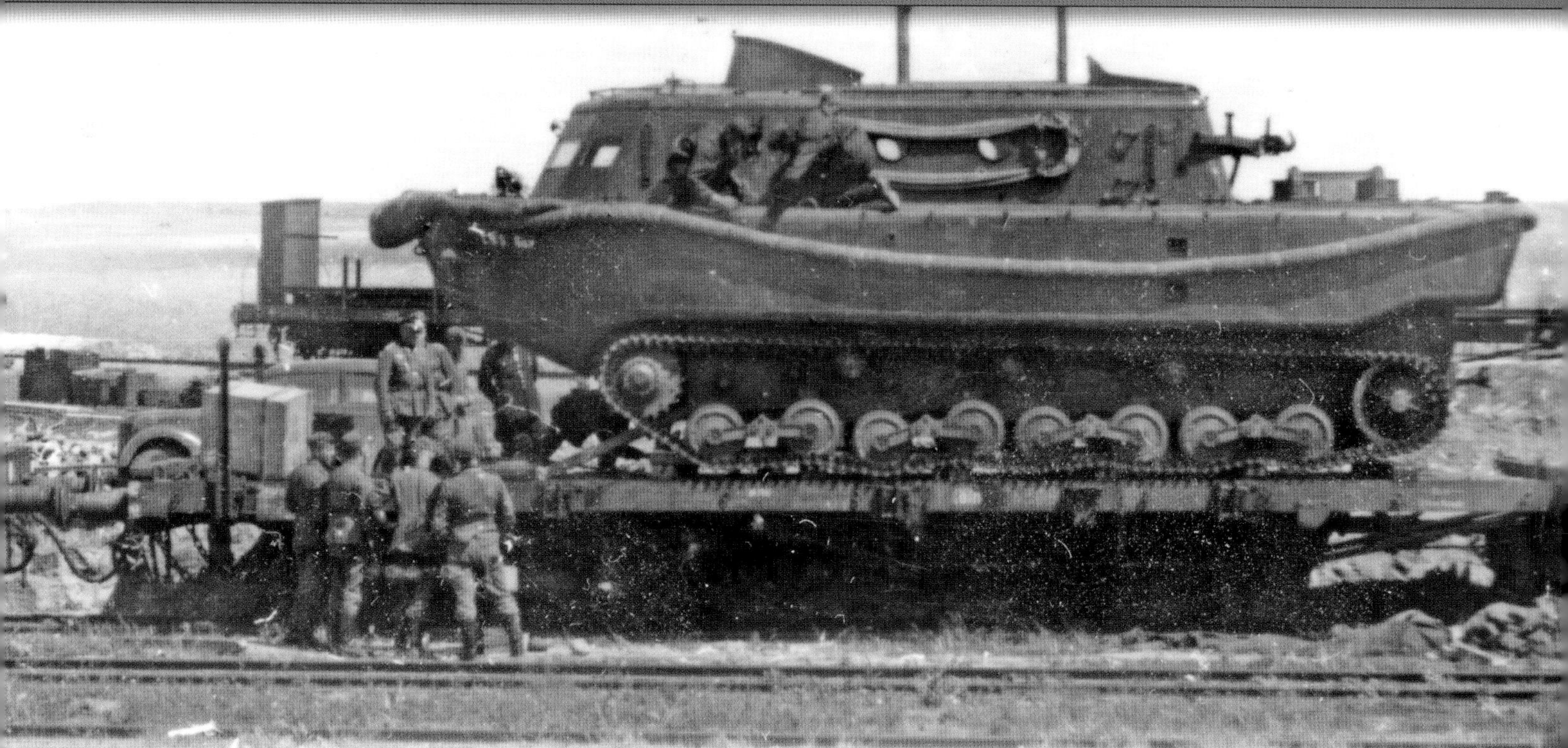

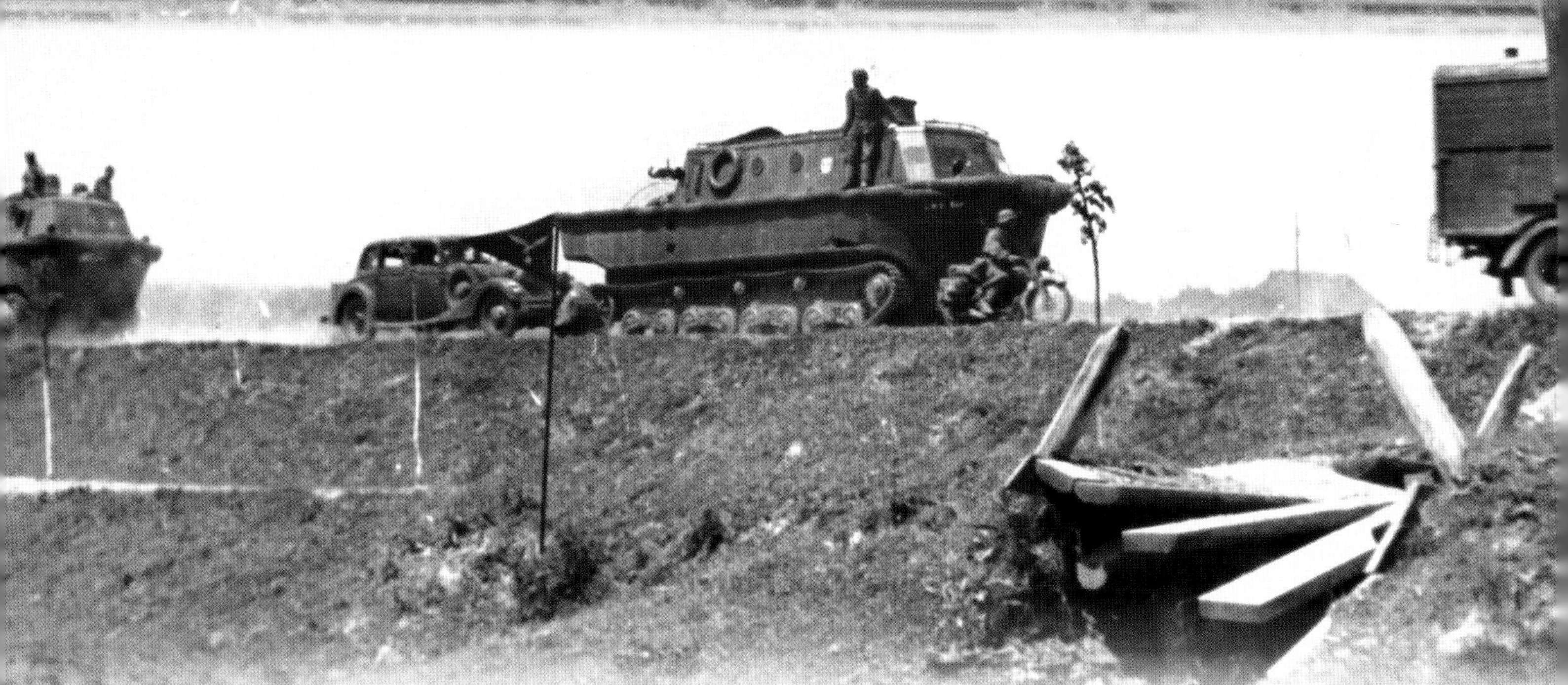

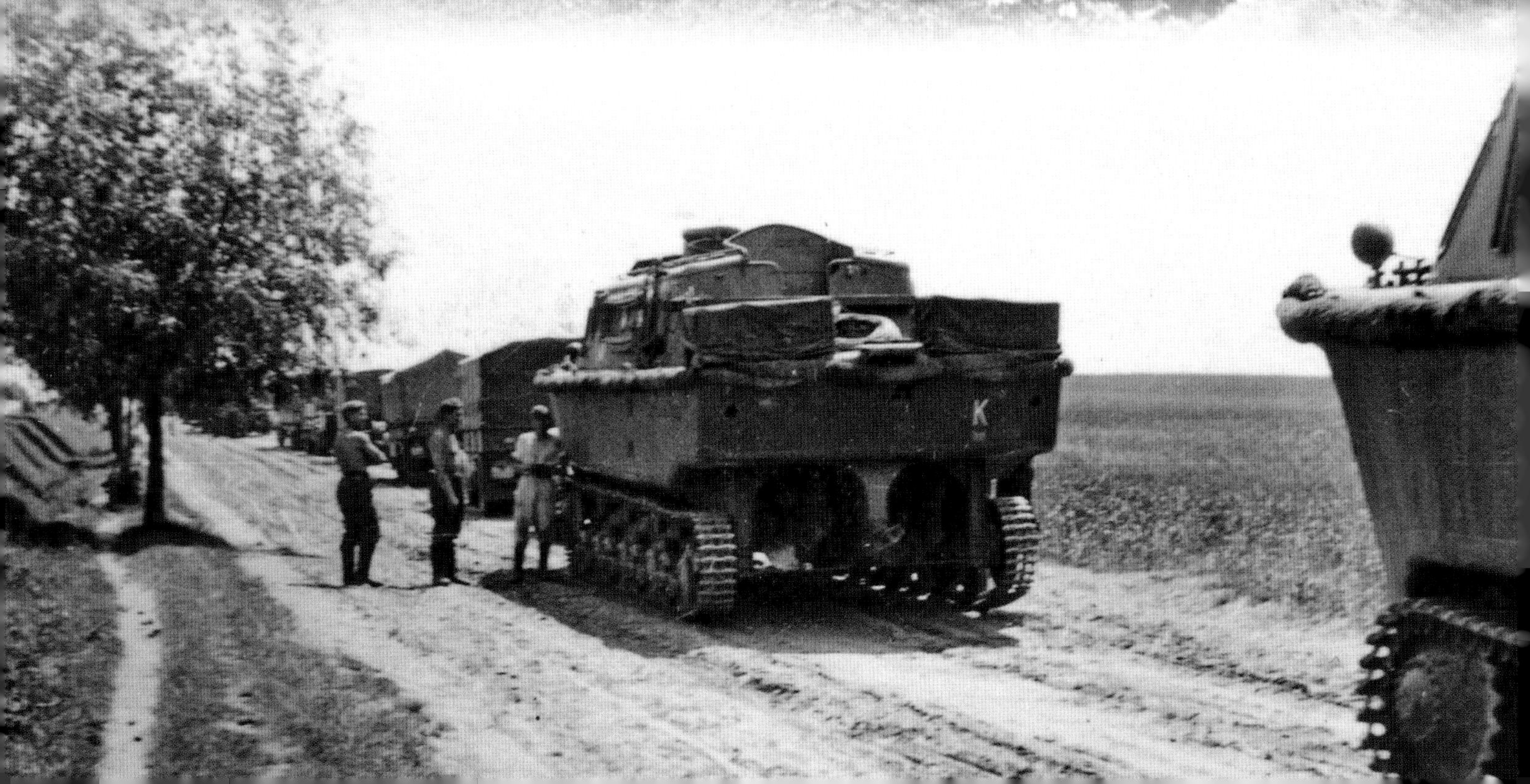

Above, below and following pages. **Three other shots of L.W.S. 6 67 in its unit taken during a stop in a Russian village. The column of three L.W.S. is rather impressive.** (Collection AMC)

Above and below. **Three other shots of the L.W.S. 6 67 towing the L.W.S. 500 26 which had broken down and which, given the number of photos taken of it while still being towed by 6 67, took a long time to repair.** *(Collection AMC)*

Above, below and next page.
Eight other photographs of the L.W.S. 6 67 in its unit on the Eastern Front; note there are a lot of tools and other equipment on the rear deck of the L.W.S.s, there being very little storage space inside. The absence of armament is particularly visible here: of the three machines, none has any machine guns, seeing as they were engineer vehicles intended for crossing rivers.
(Collection AMC)

The L.W.S. 6 67 in Sicily before leaving for Africa.

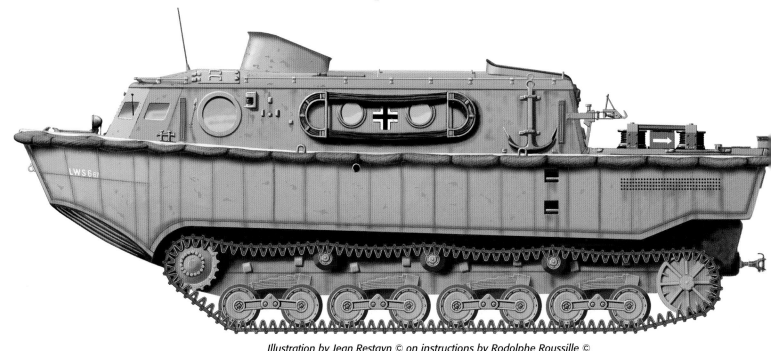

*Illustration by Jean Restayn © on instructions by Rodolphe Roussille ©
for Histoire et Collections 2012.*

**Three shots of the L.W.S.
6 67 taken in Sicily just
before its departure for
Libya. In the first two
pictures, the Pionier
Landungs-Kompanie
778 insignia was not
painted yet.**
(Collection AMC)

The L.W.S. 6 67 landing in Libya.

Illustration by Jean Restayn © on instructions by Rodolphe Roussille ©
for Histoire et Collections 2012.

Above, below and next page.
Several shots of the L.W.S 6 67 landing from a Marinefährpram in Libya near Tobruk. At that time it was assigned to the Pionier-Landungs-Kompanie 778.

(Collection AMC.)

(Bundesarchive)

(E.C.P.A.D.)

(E.C.P.A.D.)

Following pages 89 and 90. **The L.W.S. 6 67 transporting a type 40 Pionier Landungs Boot bearing the number 211. Photo taken in the north-east of Libya, eighteen or so miles from Tobruk.** (Collection AMC)

Below. **The L.W.S. 6 67 coming out of the water somewhere in Libya.**

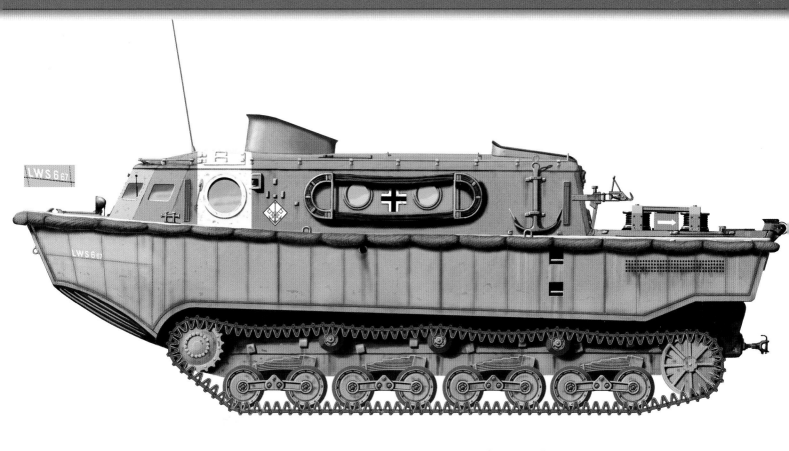

*Illustration by Jean Restayn © on instructions by Rodolphe Roussille ©
for Histoire et Collections 2012*

**Two shots of the LWS 6 67 after
it was repainted sand colour with
a white stripe on its cabin, probably
for air recognition.**
(Collection AMC)

The L.W.S. 7 68 on the eastern front

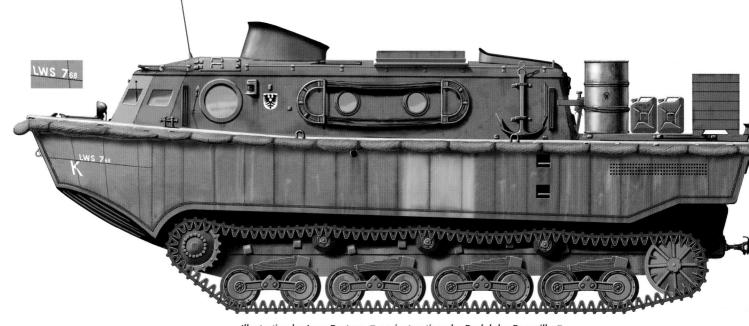

Illustration by Jean Restayn © on instructions by Rodolphe Roussille ©
for Histoire et Collections 2012.

Sources indicate that the LWS 7 68 was part of the Pionier-Landungs-Bataillon 86, and numerous photographs show it in convoys in the same unit as the L.W.S. 500 26 and 6 67. It was most likely not sent to Africa and finished its service on the Eastern Front.

Above, below and next page.
Eleven pictures of the L.W.S. 7 68 on the Eastern Front. We can easily identify this L.W.S with its big crates and oil drums lying on its rear deck. It was probably destroyed during the eastern campaign. *(Collection AMC)*

Above, opposite and following pages.
Six other photos of the L.W.S. 7 68, identical to the L.W.S. 6 67. It can be distinguished on the period photos by the large box visible on its rear deck as well as the 200 litre (45 gallons) tank.(Collection AMC)

Above, opposite and preceding page. **Four other shots of the L.W.S. 7 68 from the Pionier Bataillon 627 on the Eastern Front.** *(Collection AMC)*

Above and below.
Two other shots of the L.W.S. 7 68. The time and place these photos were taken have not been determined with any certainty. It is possible that they were photographed at the same time as the 11 72 and the Panzerfährer during exercises in the Baltic in 1943. It seems it was painted light grey at the time or more probably beige with the Balkan Kreuz clearly visible on the cabin.

The L.W.S. 10 71 on the eastern front

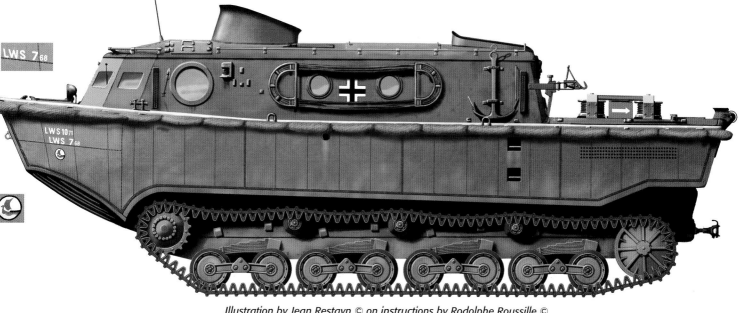

LWS 7.68

LWS 10.71
LWS 7.68

Illustration by Jean Restayn © on instructions by Rodolphe Roussille ©
for Histoire et Collections 2012.

The LWS 10 71 was assigned to the Pionier-Landungs-Bataillon 771 in April 1944. It is known in two versions: a grey version and a black, medium grey and off-white three-tone camouflage version identical to those found on Kriegsmarine ships.

Above, below and next page.
This photo report of a trial of the L.W.S 10 71 must have been taken near Vlissingen in Holland in 1940 when the LWS was attached to the Panzerabteilung F 100. *(DR)*

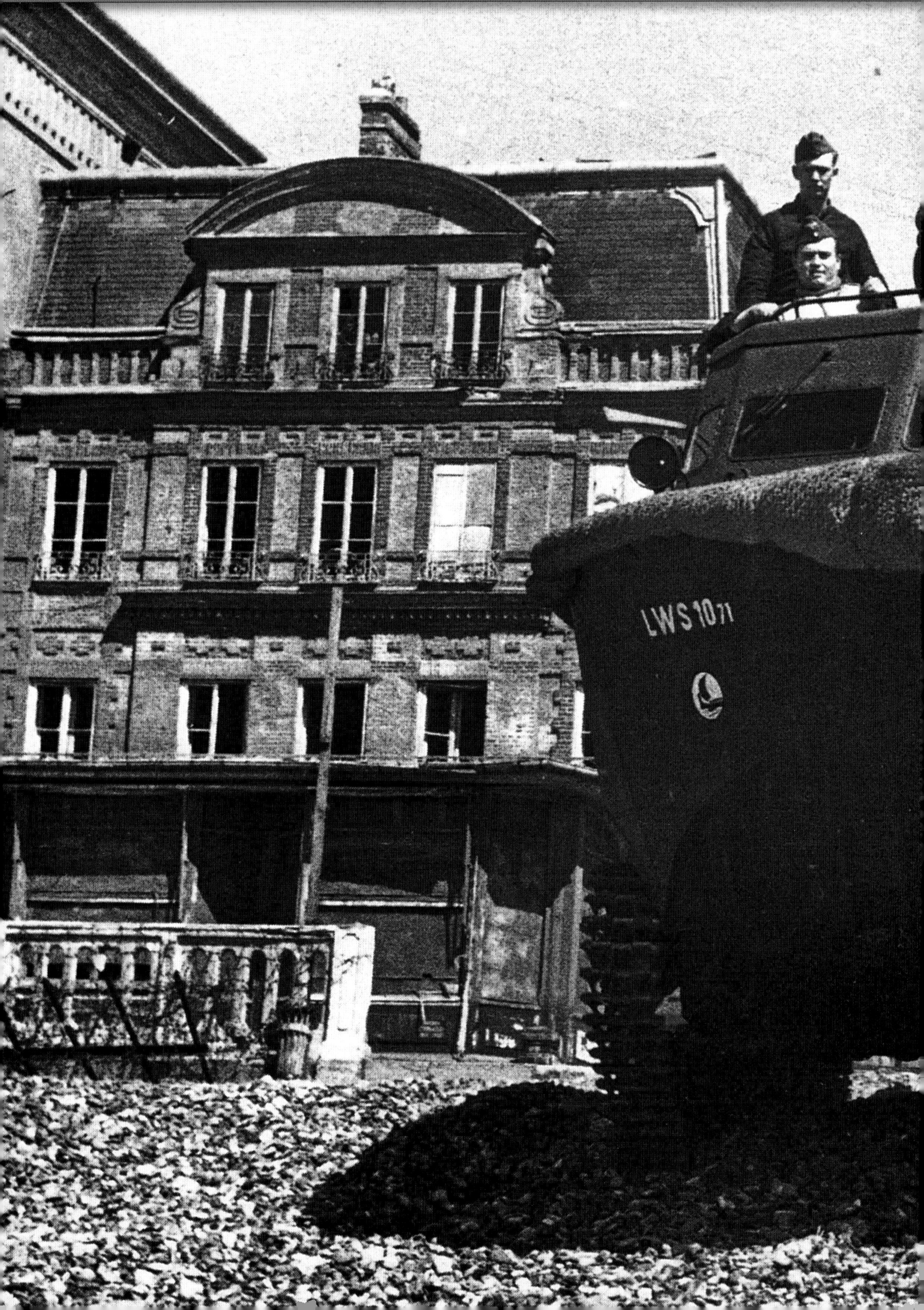
LWS 10 71

Above, below and opposite page. **Panzerabteilung F 100 was part of the unit lead by Major Wachtel of Luftwaffe Sonderkommando, who was in charge of the fitting of the landing craft (Landungsboot and Siebelfähre equipped with 8,8 cm FlaK). This affiliation explains the crew members' typical Luftwaffe uniforms and life jackets.** *(DR)*

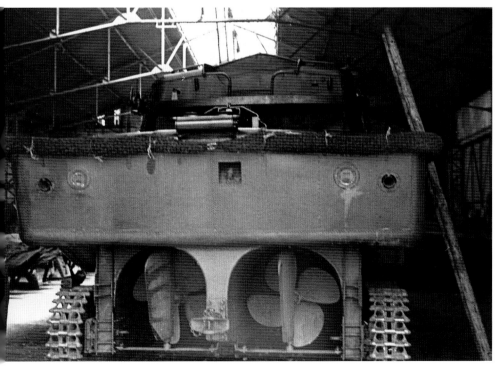

The L.W.S. 10 71 in Baltique

LWS 1071

*Illustration by Jean Restayn © on instructions by Rodolphe Roussille ©
for Histoire et Collections 2012.*

One of the rare photos of the L.W.S. 10 71 with its three colour camouflage scheme. *(DR)*

Nex page.
One of the rare photos showing the LWS 11 72 before its running gear was modified. It has only 3 return rollers. In the background we can see two L.W.S. II (Panzerfähre). *(DR)*

The final version of the L.W.S. 11 72 fitted with the late running gear with four top rollers. It is launching a midget-submarine type Molch on its special transport trailer in the sea.

The L.W.S. 11 72

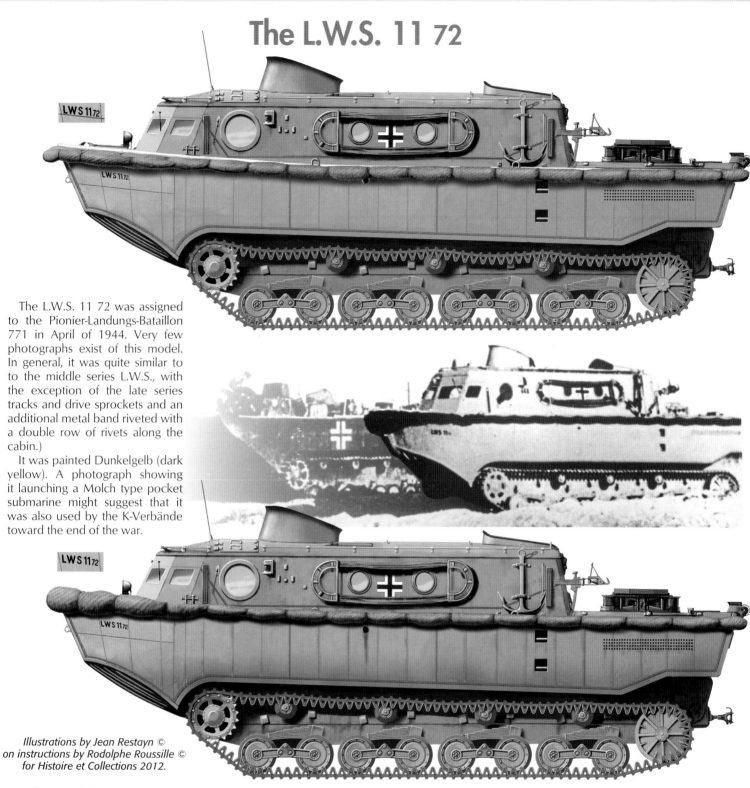

The L.W.S. 11 72 was assigned to the Pionier-Landungs-Bataillon 771 in April of 1944. Very few photographs exist of this model. In general, it was quite similar to to the middle series L.W.S., with the exception of the late series tracks and drive sprockets and an additional metal band riveted with a double row of rivets along the cabin.)

It was painted Dunkelgelb (dark yellow). A photograph showing it launching a Molch type pocket submarine might suggest that it was also used by the K-Verbände toward the end of the war.

Illustrations by Jean Restayn ©
on instructions by Rodolphe Roussille ©
for Histoire et Collections 2012.

The L.W.S. WM-29789

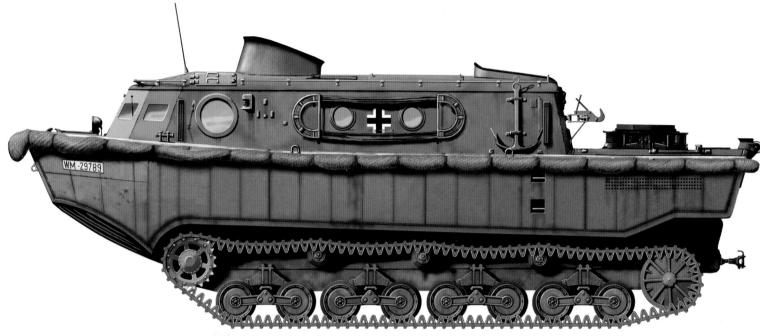

*Illustration by Jean Restayn © on instructions by Rodolphe Roussille ©
for Histoire et Collections 2012.*

While we know very little about its history, we can assume that it was assigned toward the end of the war to special units of the Kriegsmarine, the KleinkampfVerbände. These small commando units were equipped with explosive launches (Linse), human torpedoes (Neger or Marder) and pocket submarines (Molch, Biber and Seehund). These highly mobile units required an amphibious launching system; this is why they acquired the WM 29 789. Only one post-war photograph of it exists. The LWS WM-29 789 was captured by the Americans who shipped it to Aberdeen, tested its capabilities, and then sent it to be scrapped.

**The only remaining L.W.S 29 789 taken
in Aberdeen after the war.** *(DR)*

The L.W.S. WM-29792

*Illustration by Jean Restayn © on instructions by Rodolphe Roussille ©
for Histoire et Collections 2012.*

M 29792 was also assigned to the units of the K-Verband at the end of the war. It was captured by the English. This is the only proof of its existence. To this day we do not know what the letter C painted inside a white square at the front of the cabin meant.

**The only known picture of the
L.W.S 29 792 SER 235. A big C was painted
on the right front side of the cabin.**
(Collection AMC)

The L.W.S. WM-29793

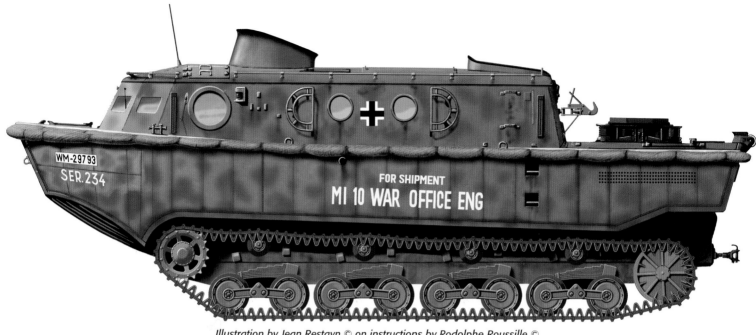

*Illustration by Jean Restayn © on instructions by Rodolphe Roussille ©
for Histoire et Collections 2012.*

**Two photos of the L.W.S. 29 793
SER 234 taken just after the war.**
(Collection Martin Mace)

IV - The L.W.S. amphibious trailers

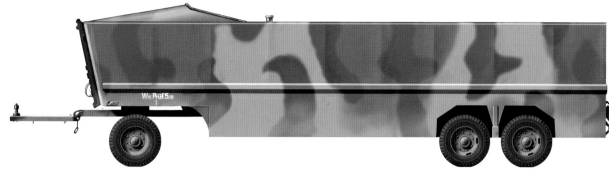

*Illustration by Jean Restayn © on instructions by Rodolphe Roussille ©
for Histoire et Collections 2012.*

In Mai 1941 Kässboher of Ulm received a demand from the Heereswaafenamt for several trailers of two different types for the Land-Wasser-Schlepper.

The design specifications indicated that the two trailers should be able to carry, as a road transporter and a ferry, payloads of 10 tons and 20 tons. According to official figures from 1942, six prototypes of amphibious trailers were delivered for evaluation: four 10-ton models and two 20-ton models. Very few pictures exist of these trailers; both types seem to have been delivered painted grey, the same colour as that used on the L.W.S.

The 10 Ton Trailer

The two trailers were very alike in appearance, the biggest difference being their running gear and the more rounded, less angular shapes of the 10 ton trailer. The 'light' 10 ton trailer had classical running gear, rims and tyres of the type found on the tank transport trailers Sd.anh 155 and 116. Two photographs of the Land-Wasser-Schlepper undergoing trials with the marking Wä.Pruf show the 10 ton trailer with three-tone camouflage patches with the classic brown, green and sand camouflage colours of German armoured vehicles.

Two shots of the 10 ton trailer with a 3 colour camouflage scheme, towed by the L.W.S. 6 67 during trials. See the WaPrüf 5 IVB inscription painted in white on the side of the trailer.
(Collection AMC).

Rear shots of the 10 ton trailer towed by the L.W.S. 6 67 or 7 68 on the Eastern Front. In this picture, we can see the two other LWS of the unit. In the foreground is LWS 500 26.
(Collection AMC).

Three shots of the 10 ton amphibious trailer built by Kässbohrer.
The 10 ton trailer has tires and rims. In these pictures the colour of the trailer is probably medium grey.
(Collection NARA).

The 20 Ton Trailer

The 20 ton trailer had solid rubber wheels, the same as those found on the heavy tank transport trailer manufactured by Culemeyer. The running gear of the 20 ton trailer had the added oddity of being removable, probably to facilitate its transport by railroad. Contemporary sources indicate that the 20 tons trailer measured 9,960 x 3,110 x 2,950 mm. It could carry all types of vehicle up to the 18 ton SD.Kfz. 9 Famo half-track tractor. The water depth was 1,450 mm and the trailer weighed 12.3 tons.

These are the only two known photos of the 20 ton amphibious trailer being towed. It is being towed by an early type Land-Wasser-Schlepper. *(Collection AMC).*

Photos of the 20 ton trailer with an 18 ton Sd.kfz 9 Famo half-track being loaded. This trailer was designed for loads up to 20 tons.
(Collection NARA).

Illustration by Jean Restayn © on instructions by Rodolphe Roussille © for Histoire et Collections 2012.

Left an right.
Two shots of 20 tons amphibious trailer on a Reichbahn flatbed railway car. When loaded onto the railway car, wheels were removed in order to decrease the total height. *(Collection NARA).*

Shot of a 20 tons amphibious trailer in water. *(Collection NARA).*

V - The L.W.S. II (PANZERFÄHRE)

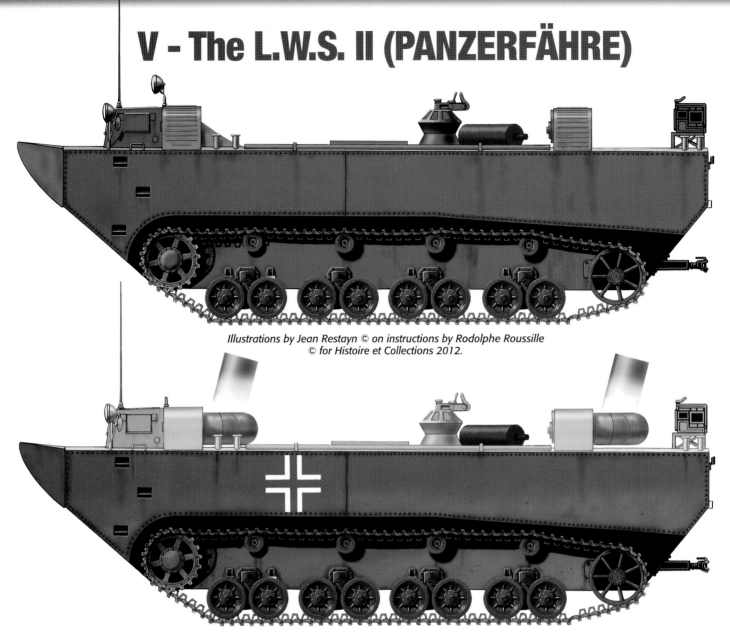

Illustrations by Jean Restayn © on instructions by Rodolphe Roussille
© for Histoire et Collections 2012.

In April 1941 Wa Prüf IVb signed a contract with Magirus to study the development of a light armoured version of the Land-Wasser-Schlepper under the code name of LWS II (also known by the name of Panzerfähre, literally translated as armoured ferry).

The objective of this project was to provide the army with the basic means to carry out river crossings for light and medium tanks, like the Panzer IV, without having to rely on a system of pontoon bridges. As with the construction of the Land-Wasser-Schlepper, several companies were involved in the development of the project, among them Krupp-Gruson AG for the supply of the two Panzer IV chassis, ZF, Maybach for the engines, and Kässbohrer for the superstructure and the amphibious trailer that went with it. The idea at the beginning of the project was to create a combination of amphibious tractors joined together by a transport pontoon capable of accommodating a Panzer for river crossings. This floating platform system was joined to the two Panzerfähre by triangular attachments made of metal tubes.

The first vehicle built in the Magirus plant. It used the running gear of the Panzer IV. *(Collection NARA).*

A pre-study model of the Panzerfähre prototype.

The construction of the first two prototypes was launched in July 1941 and they were delivered for evaluation ten months later in May of '42. The Panzerfähre were rigorously tested during the following twelve months. However, the results of these tests were a disappointment as the performance of the Panzerfähre did not live up to the expectations of the High Command.

The real weakness of the system was the instability of the platform and the buoyancy of the Panzerfähre combination.

You only need to take a quick look at the photographs taken during the tests to be convinced of the precariousness of this instable combination. Also, the introduction into service of new heavy tanks such as the Panther followed by the Tiger I and II completely changed the equation. In fact, the worthwhileness of such a system was called into question. It would have required the development of an even more power LWS III with an over-sized transport pontoon. The project ended here, and for the rest of the war all river crossings were carried out by different pontoon systems, which have yet to be the subject of a serious study. According to some sources, the two Panzerfähre were involved in the fighting near Wolgast in the fighting in 1945 near Wolgast, a German town in western Mecklenburg-Pomerania. The two vehicles were sunk at Negenmarkerinne and then salvaged a few months later, at the end of '45 by the Soviets for the study and conception of their own post-war amphibious vehicles.

This is the chassis of L.W.S. II, with the Panzer IV Maybach HL 120 engine.
(Collection NARA).

Technical characteristics of the Panzerfähre

Contrary to the singular design of the Land-Wasser-Schlepper which was entirely made up of specific parts (with the exception of a few parts taken from the Panzerkampfwagen II: rear wheels and tracks for the first version and production version), the Panzerfähre used the same chassis as the Panzer IV auf. A. The hull was also much simpler than that of the LWS. Instead of having a complex boat-shaped hull, the superstructure of the Panzerfähre was made up of sharp angles with no curves, and resembled a covered pontoon more than a boat. The superstructure was made up of metal sheets, 14.5mm thick, riveted to a frame of metal beams. Small windows were drilled in the forward compartment;

these could be protected by armoured plates in combat. The LWS II possessed four tiltable air intakes on its roof, two exhaust pipes, and a rather large winch. The crew had a forward cabin which could accommodate four men who entered the vehicle through the roof by way of a hatch located on top of the forward compartment.

For its part, the transport pontoon was made up of four floating boxes attached together by steel fasteners and kept in place by safety locks. The pontoon was attached to the two Panzerfähre by tubular sections and was doubly secured by large linked metal chains, similar to those used on a bicycle.

L.W.S. II (Panzerfähre)

Technical Details
Engine type: Maybach HL 120 TRM
Number of Cylinders: 12
Maximum Output: 300 hp
Maximum speed on land: 45 km/h
Maximum speed in water: 12.5 km/h
Length: 8,250 mm
Width: 2,800 mm
Height: 2,500 mm
Maximum trailer load: 30 tons
Average fuel consumption: 90l/h

During the same trials; this image, taken from behind, shows two L.W.S. II. It is entering the water with a prototype bridge layer, developed from the Panzer IV chassis, on its transport pontoon.
(*Collection NARA*)

*Illustration by Jean Restayn © on instructions by Rodolphe Roussille ©
for Histoire et Collections 2012.*

Above and below. **Due to its poor
flotation, the LWS II had to be used in
calm rivers, not on the sea.**
(Collection NARA)

*Illustration by Jean Restayn © on instructions by Rodolphe Roussille ©
for Histoire et Collections 2012.*

Above and below. **A Panzerfähre towing the amphibious trailer. Actually, the trailer itself was not amphibious but merely a platform with wheels used to carry
the parts of the Panzerfähre pontoon. Unlike the LWS
amphibious trailers, the Panzerfähre trailer could not
carry materials or vehicles.**
(Collection NARA)

Two shots of two Panzerfähre prototypes. One, fitted with its rear crane system, is removing a Maybach HL 120 engine from the second Panzerfähre. *(Collection NARA).*

Several shots of a combination of two Panzerfähre with their transport pontoon during trials. This combination was supposed to becapable of carrying medium Panzers from one bank of a river to the other. These two are the late versions of the Panzerfähre. The top corner of the hull has been angled for better water penetration. *(Collection NARA).*

Below. **One of the rare views of the Panzerfähre painted in dark yellow.** *(Collection AMC).*

VI - L.W.S. III (Skoda LR.30)

The history of this interesting, but little known vehicle began during the second half of the Second World War. This project was conceived in the context of replacing the Land-Wasser-Schlepper I and II. The impetus for the development of this vehicle came from the Waffen SS, and more specifically the SS Technical Academy. The promotion of this project was provided by the commander of the academy, Professor of Engineering SS Brigadeführer General Major Gerloff, who secured the support of a Wehrmacht general belonging to the HwaA-WaPrüf 5, Lieutenant General Jod, as well as the Ministry of Industry run by Speer. On paper, the project started with serious financial and logistical support, in terms of the generous allocation of manpower and materials. The Czech company Skoda was entrusted with the design and construction of the new amphibious vehicle. They, in turn, passed the project on to their subsidiary Blizen Automobile Section No. 83. The project was launched under the code A 1-33, but the designation was chaotic and diverse and the code changed throughout its duration. More often than not, the project was known as Project "Schwimmfährig". The Waffen SS committee in charge of the contract with the Directorate General of Škoda used another name: the Škoda Landwasserschlmpper LR 30. The Czech name for the project was much simpler since the project was called "floating tank". Post-war it was known as "heavy transport tracked amphibious vehicle LR.30".

The project was constantly confronted with a lack of raw materials, equipment and tools, and the Czech engineers were forced to use parts from other vehicles in production. The objective was to standardise the components as much as possible, thus allowing for easier maintenance. HwaA-WaPrüf 5 in particular emphasised the design of the engine, transmission and running gear. Škoda refused, arguing that without specific construction parts for the LR. 30 it would be impossible to achieve the desired performance results. For a time this argument convinced the SS general staff, but the project was abruptly stopped in the first half of 1944. The exact reasons for this are nowhere to be found, and, in any case, at that time Skoda would not have had the raw materials or the parts necessary to develop the first prototype.

The design of this vehicle, which was to remain a "panzer-paper", was very interesting. The LR.30 was powered by two engines located at the rear, a main V12, 450 hp, gasoline engine and a secondary V4 50 hp gasoline engine. The secondary engine was located next to the main engine and was used to power a pump system which started the main engine. The design of the chassis and propulsion system was inspired by, though not identical to, the Škoda T-25 tank. The drive sprocket was situated at the front and the running gear had ten double rollers of 550 mm in diameter.

The vehicle, which depending on variants could theoretically weigh up to 30 tons, was probably intended for transport and supply and had to be amphibious. To make it float, it had two removable side floating chambers. Once on land, the LR 30 could raise its chambers to make it more maneuverable, detach them, or tow them on a specially designed trailer. Once in an aquatic environment, the LWS III was equipped with two propellers of 600 mm in diameter with a maximum of 1,000 rpm. On land, tracks of 700 mm in width ensured the stability of this imposing machine. The vehicle was a transport vehicle, and, as such, was not armoured. Like the LWS and Panzerfähre, it did not have any weapons. It had a large opening on its roof but of larger dimensions, 4 metres by 1.5 metres.

There is no trace in the official documentation as to the specific use that the Waffen SS had in mind for the vehicle. The intention was probably to use the vehicle for resupply of troops over difficult terrain and possibly for Special Forces missions (infiltration, sabotage etc....)

The end point of the project was marked by the Allied bombardment of the plant on May 4, 1945, during which all the project documentation and a wooden model, scale 1:10, went up in flames. ∎

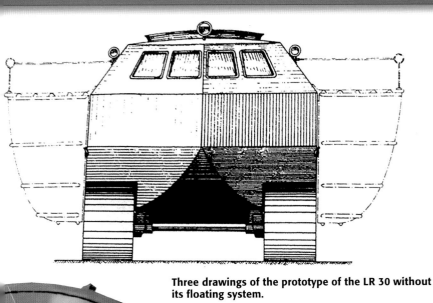
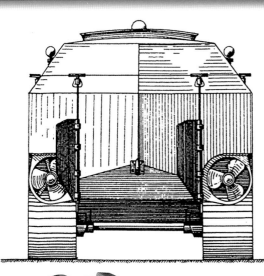

Three drawings of the prototype of the LR 30 without its floating system.

The wood 1/10 scale model of the L.W.S. III (Skoda LR.30) with its floaters in sailing position.

The back of the LR.30 in sailing configuration. We can see the two 70 mm diameter propellers.

21

Artist view of the model but this time the floaters are raised for land transport. *(Coloured drawing by Jean Restayn)*

Two shots of the L.W.S III model tested in water. We can see the two large openings on the roof.

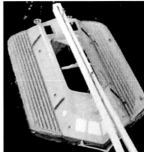

Technical Details
Weight : 27 tonnes (25.5 tonnes without the flotation chambers)
Engine : 2 x Škoda (450 hp + 50 hp)
Main air-cooled engine : V12
Maximum yield : 320 kW
Secondary engine : V4
Maximum speed on land : 25 km/h
Autonomy : 5 hours
Maximum speed in water : 8 km/h
Measurable surface pressure : 0.685 kg/cm²
Maximum gradient : 25°
Floating capacity without the floatation chambers : 1 m
Diameter of the propellers : 700 mm
Crew : 4 men   Maximum payload: 30 tonnes

UM075 LWS Captain

UM077 LWS Crew N°1

UM078 LWS Crew N°2

UM078 LWS Crew N°2

UM76 LWS Driver

UM94 LWS Crew N°4

UM93 LWS Crew N°3

UM95 LWS Crew N°5

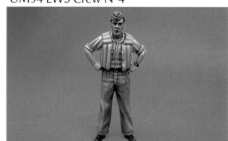
UM134 LWS Crew N°6

UM134 LWS/Panzerfähre Crew N°7

UM139 Panzerfähre Crew N°2

UM083 LWS accessories set N°3

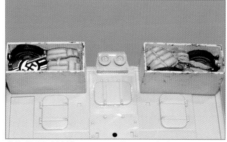
UM082 LWS accessories set N°2

UM071 LWS bumpers

UM073 LWS accessories set

UM074 LWS update set for Bronco kit

UM100 LWS 10 tons amphibious trailer

126

 Human torpedo pilot n°1

 Human torpedo pilot n°2

 Human torpedo pilot n°3

 Midget submarine pilot n°1

 Midget submarine pilot n°3

 Sprengboot Linse pilot

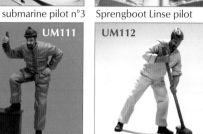 Sprengboot Linse crew

Midget submarine pilot n°2

U-boat/ S-boat Captain

U-boat/ S-boat sailor

U-boat/S-boat sailor

S-Boat/U-boat sweeping

-Boat/ U-boat crew with a bucket | S-Boat/ U-boat smoking | S-Boat/ U-boat officer n°2 | U-boat commander at rest n°2 | S-Boat/ U-boat crew at rest n°2 | S-Boat/ U-boat crew at rest n°3

 -Boat/ U-boat officer n°3

 S-Boat/ U-boat crew at rest n°4

 S-Boat/ U-boat crew n°1

 S-Boat/ U-boat officer n°1

 S-Boat / U-boat crew n°2

 S-Boat / U-boat crew n°3

 -Boat/ U-boat crew n°4

 S-Boat/ U-boat officer n°2

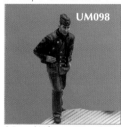 S-Boat/ U-boat crew n°5

 S-Boat/ U-boat crew n°6

 WWII German truck driver

 WWII Kriegsmarine life-jackets

 US Sailor n°1

 US Sailor n°2

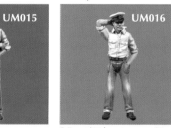 S-Boat/ U-boat crew n°5

 US Navy sailor at rest n°4

 US Navy sailor and officer smoking

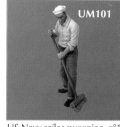 US Navy sailor sweeping n°1

 S Navy sailor sweeping n°2

 US Navy sailor with a bucket / US Navy sailor at rest n°5

 US Sailor at rest n°1

 US Sailor at rest n°2

 US Sailor at rest n°3

 Royal Navy sailor n°4

 S Navy Captain n°2

 US Navy captain n°3 / US Tankers at rest smoking / WWII Us Navy life-jackets / Royal Navy sailor n°3

UM004 German type Hecht midget-submarine

UM025 German type Delphin midget-submarine

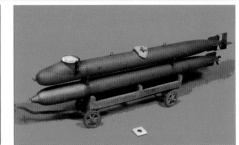
UM024 Neger-Marder accessories

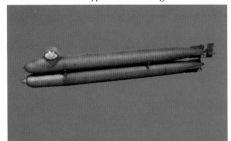
UM021 German type Neger human torpedo

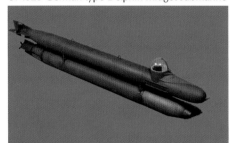
UM022 German type Marder human torpedo

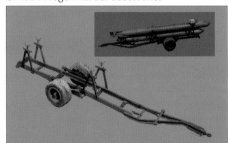
UM023 Neger / Marder trailer

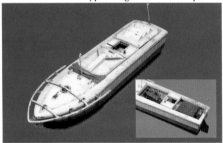
UM029 Sprengboot Linse (explosive boat)

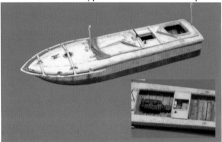
UM026 Kommandoboot Linse (explosive boat)

UM141 Biber Midget submarine transport trailer

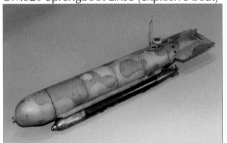
UM143 Molch Midget submarine

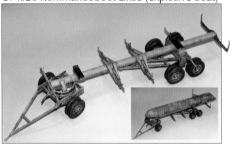
UM144 Molch Midget submarine transport trailer

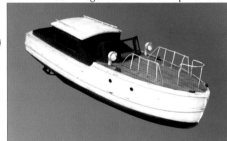
UM041 Kreigsmarine Barkasse / Luftwaffe rescue boat

UM107 Tupolev Danube overcraft

UM105 Locotracteur Billard

UM106 Wagon Péchot

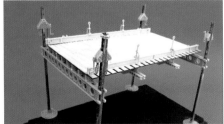
UM123 WWII German trestle bridge section

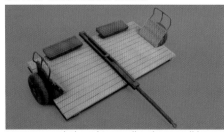
UM142 Arado beaching trolley for Revell kit

UM146 WWII German electric crane

128

UM122 LCVP blindé convertion for Italeri

UM127 to UM131 Indochina LCVP Blindé Crew